Lead without Blame

LEAD WITHOUT BLAME

BUILDING RESILIENT LEARNING TEAMS

DIANA LARSEN
TRICIA BRODERICK

CONTRIBUTION BY
GILMARA VILA NOVA-MITCHELL

BK®

Berrett–Koehler Publishers, Inc.

Berrett-Koehler Publishers, Inc.
1333 Broadway, Suite 1000
Oakland, CA 94612-1921
Tel: (510) 817-2277   Fax: (510) 817-2278   www.bkconnection.com

Ordering Information
Quantity sales. Special discounts are available on quantity purchases by corporations, associations, and others. For details, contact the "Special Sales Department" at the Berrett-Koehler address above.
Individual sales. Berrett-Koehler publications are available through most bookstores. They can also be ordered directly from Berrett-Koehler: Tel: (800) 929-2929; Fax: (802) 864-7626; www.bkconnection.com.
Orders for college textbook / course adoption use. Please contact Berrett-Koehler: Tel: (800) 929-2929; Fax: (802) 864-7626.

Distributed to the U.S. trade and internationally by Penguin Random House Publisher Services.

Berrett-Koehler and the BK logo are registered trademarks of Berrett-Koehler Publishers, Inc.

Printed in Canada

Berrett-Koehler books are printed on long-lasting acid-free paper. When it is available, we choose paper that has been manufactured by environmentally responsible processes. These may include using trees grown in sustainable forests, incorporating recycled paper, minimizing chlorine in bleaching, or recycling the energy produced at the paper mill.

Library of Congress Cataloging-in-Publication Data

Names: Larsen, Diana, author. | Broderick, Tricia, author.
Title: Lead without blame : building resilient learning teams / Diana Larsen, Tricia
   Broderick, Gilmara Vila Nova-Mitchell ; contribution by Gilmara Vila Nova-Mitchell.
Description: First Edition. | Oakland, CA : Berrett-Koehler Publishers, [2022] | Includes
   bibliographical references and index.
Identifiers: LCCN 2022010153 (print) | LCCN 2022010154 (ebook) |
   ISBN 9781523000548 (paperback) | ISBN 9781523000555 (pdf) |
   ISBN 9781523000562 (epub) | ISBN 9781523000579
Subjects: LCSH: Teams in the workplace. | Organizational learning. |
   Employee motivation. | Leadership.
Classification: LCC HD66 .L367 2022 (print) | LCC HD66 (ebook) | DDC 658.4/
   022—dc23/eng/20220228
LC record available at https://lccn.loc.gov/2022010153
LC ebook record available at https://lccn.loc.gov/2022010154

First Edition
30 29 28 27 26 25 24 23 22   10 9 8 7 6 5 4 3 2 1

Book production: Westchester Publishing Services
Cover design: Adam Johnson

I dedicate this book to my grandchildren, Jackson Spear, Tündér Larsen, and River Larsen. And to everyone who accepts the challenge of conceiving and establishing workplaces where everyone in every part can thrive. Let's collaborate to give our children and grandchildren the enriching work and work environments they deserve.

—Diana Larsen

I dedicate this book to the late David Hussman. He viewed every problem as an opportunity to explore with endless passion and curiosity. I carry this and more with me. And whenever I do hesitate, I can hear him saying, "You got this, sister!" I made a promise to David to keep paying help forward. I hope this book honors that promise.

—Tricia Broderick

Contents

Figures and Tables

Foreword

A few years ago, I invited my extended leadership team to attend a weeklong leadership workshop. During a break, I was having a conversation with one of the co-trainers, Tricia Broderick, about my leadership failures. A few minutes before the conversation, I'd just completed a failure bow. I was acknowledging my fault in the slow execution of a change that was critically important to the success of our organization. At the time, I was very focused on how I was failing to create a strong and supportive context for the team and to support more team autonomy. Tricia said to me, "Van, you know your ability to publicly admit your failures is your superpower." I thought, "Superpower? What is she talking about?" And just like that, I shifted from thinking about what I was doing wrong to what more I could do to help. Could I use this superpower for more? Did I have other superpowers that might be useful?

As I write this, I am almost midway through my first year as the vice president of information technology of the 40-plus-billion-dollar enterprise that is the University of California. I am leading an organization that has 8,000 IT professionals supporting teaching, research, health care, and investing.

Previously, I had been leading a much smaller organization through a difficult agile transformation. My entire organization was unfamiliar with agile. My relatively new leadership team was still struggling with burnout caused by lack of trust in each other and our teams, an inability to engage in constructive conflict, and pressure from me to make major changes happen while still trying to align on the goals. Through her intense curiosity, wisdom, humor, experience, insight, and compassion, Tricia managed to unlock something inside me and my team: our ability to work effectively as a high-performing team and our shared passion for cultivating other high-performing teams within our organization.

Later, I encountered Diana Larsen and her ideas. And I have been a fan ever since. Diana is an expert at helping you to deconstruct the steps necessary for people to move from groups to teams that consistently deliver value. She's someone who manages to find the way and the words to make it simple to take teams through successful lift-offs that are oriented around vision, mission, and shared social contracts to a place where they aren't just consistently delivering business value; they are consistently optimizing their delivery of that value.

They have both taught me lessons that are used every day. I've learned the importance of openly cultivating my curiosity for learning in ways that support my teams. I've learned how to model vulnerability, demonstrate compassion for my team as we learn, and offer visible and vocal confidence in my team's ability to learn and execute. In this book, you will learn these skills and more through a framework that will help you be a learning leader in the increasingly volatile, uncertain, complex, and ambiguous world that we all now live in.

What Diana Larsen and Tricia Broderick have put into *Lead without Blame: Building Resilient Learning Teams* is a framework for the change needed in yourself to help create and nurture high-performing, resilient learning teams. It is a framework that I wish I had years ago, because it clearly and eloquently breaks down the principles needed in leadership to shift from blaming to learning, and it connects those principles seamlessly with tools we need to support resilient teams that are tightly aligned and continuously learning. It does that by showing you how to strengthen your team's inclusivity while minimizing power dynamics.

While certainly not prescriptive, the book ties together real-world research with experience gained through coaching, mentoring, teaching, and leading a wide variety of organizations in order to help you design and structure your team and its ways of working to avoid the pitfalls of activity instead of progress and of bottlenecks and dependencies instead of autonomy and agility.

For teams and leaders, the last several years have been a roller coaster of pandemics and prejudices, digital boom, and baleful digital divides. Never has there been a time when resilient teams are needed more. There has been too much of a shift to technology as a connecting factor. It is not the technology that has allowed us to be resilient and connected. It is our desire as human beings to connect; our ability as friends, family, and colleagues to empathize; our skills as professionals in helping each and every one to be seen. Sometimes this happens when we turn out the lights to allow everyone to see how the sparks in the darkness shine, and sometimes it happens when we create the space for quiet so that we can hear the whispers of beautiful butterfly wings. Although the contents of this book are timeless, the moment we are in also makes them timely.

I believe this book will be as transformational for you as my initial encounter with its ideas were for me. If you are ready to lead through learning, this book is for you. If you are ready to lead resilient learning teams that thrive in the face of adversity and complexity, this is the book for you. All of our worlds have become more complex. In the face of that complexity, I hope this book inspires you as much as it has inspired me to be courageous, confident, and compassionate with yourself and your teams.

Enjoy the journey!

Van Williams
Vice President, IT
University of California

Foreword

When companies hire me, it's usually because they're a bit stuck on a problem. Anco (a fictional name) was no different. Anco was working on a new product and the development teams were falling behind schedule. During my first visit, one of the vice presidents expressed his frustration: "Why aren't those teams accountable?" he asked, chopping one hand hard into his open palm. It was clear he didn't really expect an answer. It was equally clear from the syllables he emphasized that he was blaming the teams for all the problems and schedule overruns.

As I spent more time at Anco, I learned there were a number of variations on this theme. All involved blaming some other person or group—usually lower in the hierarchy. VPs did it. Directors did it, managers did it. Even Scrum Masters did it. I also noticed that lack of follow-through was pervasive at all levels, not just the teams tasked with creating products and delivering services.

More importantly, I observed that once a leader made a blaming statement, *learning and problem solving ceased.* This is not surprising. It is part of the blame dynamic.

On the other side of the dynamic, people tried to *avoid* blame. They shaded disappointing project information. They said Yes to work they knew they don't have capacity for—because they didn't want to be blamed as lazy slackers. Information became unreliable because people feared saying what was really going on. Relationships suffered. Time people might have spent solving problems and imagining new ways to do things got sucked up in "CYA" activities.

Everything is harder in the face of blame.

In the short term, it may feel satisfying to find the wringable neck. However, in the long run blaming suppresses learning, creativity, innovation—and productivity.

Why do people blame when it is so obviously costly? To some extent, blame is a habit. Managers have been taught to hold people accountable—which often means blaming them. They've been taught to find fault with individuals rather than look at systems. But blame is not inevitable.

Changing habits isn't easy. That's where *Lead without Blame* comes in. Diana and Tricia have written a guide for making the shift from traditional practices, toward leadership that creates an environment for learning.

Changing habits involves making different choices and taking different actions. That means *thinking* differently. Thinking differently about the nature of knowledge work and the workers. Thinking differently about what motivates teams and how a leader's actions contribute to—or hinder—learning. New understandings open different choices for action.

Diana and Tricia have brought together research and experience that provide insights into the nature of leadership and how leaders contribute to creating learning environments. They walk through what motivates teams, and team learning. They lay out how teams develop from a group of individuals to become co-intelligent and capable of solving tougher problems and facing greater challenges. It's a different lens that opens options.

So, thinking differently leads to acting differently. The opposite is also true. Sometimes by *acting* differently people start to *think* differently. This is one reason why well-run, blame-free retrospectives are so important in shifting the blame dynamic. They give people experience in facing problems and messes without blame. They create the belief that it is possible to bring up issues and talk about what is really happening. Through retrospectives people experience handling disappointments (and triumphs) as opportunities to understand the system, try new approaches, and learn.

Throughout the book Tricia and Diana share little vignettes that illustrate the costs of blame and how simple shifts can make a difference. These are stories that many readers will relate to. It may be that you'll recognize your own mistake. Or that you'll see yourself in a compassionate response that bolstered safety in your group. These stories bring the theories and models to life.

Moving away from blame won't be easy. Blame is deeply entrenched in many, many organizations. Even as you change your leadership style, others around you will still be stuck in blame.

However, with Tricia and Diana as your guides, you can make a start. You can start the virtuous cycle in your organization. As you change your style, you'll show that something other than blame is possible—and that it works. That will create more space for those around you to learn. Which will bring more life and creativity. Which will lead to better results—which will get more people interested. A virtuous circle.

Are you ready? Keep reading.

Esther Derby
Consultant and author of
7 Rules for Positive Productive Change:
Micros Shifts, Macro Results

Preface

In our work, we see leaders who expect results by demanding accountability. We hear it all the time, "What can I do to hold them accountable?" or "How do I convince them to take accountability for this?" We also see this approach failing, time after time. This reliance on pretending to guarantee results with judgment doesn't work. This only leads to "blame game" behaviors that cause havoc for everyone involved. In today's world, blame does not fit the work, the marketplace, or the expectations of the talent pool.

The type of glue used on post-it-notes was originally a mistake. Imagine blaming the inventor for the mistake, instead of embracing his invention. — Tweet inspired by comments in our workshop at the Agile2021 online conference[1]

Leaders want to achieve results. Yet they often miss opportunities to help their teams thrive in uncertainty and chaos. In our experience, high-performing teams excel in obvious, complicated, and complex conditions. They bring solid teamwork and understanding of the deliverables. Yet we've seen them fall apart as complexity further increases or in chaotic situations. Disruption, chaos, and uncertainty are becoming the norm, not the exception.

High-performing teams can level up by building resiliency. They've discovered how to collaboratively learn their way forward. This book highlights how to lead without blame by focusing on the essential motivators and resilience factors.

Obvious: Where everything is known upfront.

Complicated: Where the unknowns can be listed and addressed.

Complex: Where there are unknown unknowns.

Chaotic: Where the focus is to establish order and stability.

Disorder: Where there is no clarity about which of the other domains apply. —Cynefin[2]

Why We Wrote This Book Together

One day in the fall of 2020, we responded to encouragement to collaborate on a project. We began exploring our areas of shared interests. We found similarities in our backgrounds and enthusiasms. We both grew up in the Midwest states of America. We both moved west. We both had served on the board of directors of the Agile Alliance. We both shared a passion for healthy workplaces that support engaged, productive teams. We both valued collaborative relationships. And we both were looking for a partner to coauthor a new book.

While we had similarities, we also had significant differences and strengths. Our intergenerational viewpoints came from entering the work world in different decades. We have different educational backgrounds, which added to our interdisciplinary views on content. Tricia's recent corporate leadership experience provided an invaluable resource of thought. Diana's years in consulting gave her an overview of a variety of organizational cultures. For example, Tricia adds an executive perspective on shifting away from blame. And Diana carries a strong message about the shift from knowledge work to learning work.

Together, we bring this book to you. We believe in the untapped potential of leaders. We filled our writing with deep hope to inspire leaders to make a difference.

Who This Book Is For

Given the authors' backgrounds, readers might expect that we'd focus specifically on the agile community. What's the agile connection to resilient learning teams? Are teams practicing agile easier to transform into resilient learning teams? We believe the contents of this book can be extremely helpful for agile leaders. Our vision for readers is broader, though. We wrote this book for every courageous leader.

We wrote it for leaders who understand that success lies in creating a workplace where others thrive, no matter how chaotic the conditions. We find these leaders at all levels of the organization and across all specializations. We include leaders with formal titles and those with informal influence. We want every leader to be able to say, "I love my work. I have the best job ever." And we want leaders to help create environments where others say it too.

Who Helped Us

We knew from the outset of writing this book that we would be proactive in seeking feedback. Particularly, we sought a collaborator who could identify unconscious biases in our writing. We are grateful to Gilmara Vila Nova-Mitchell, a diversity, equity, and inclusion consultant. We credit Gilmara as a contributing author for Chapter 7 and a sensitivity editor for the book. Our content benefited immeasurably from her collaborations. She provided valuable insights, feedback, and perspectives on the content, and she took care to ensure that we understood each change, allowing us to grow as leaders too.

In the appreciations section at the end of this book, we acknowledge the people who helped with reviews and feedback. We couldn't have produced this book without them.

How This Book Is Organized

As you explore the contents of this book, you'll find we've organized it into two parts.

Part One includes an examination of the significance of three essential motivators that help leaders build teams: purpose, autonomy, and co-intelligence. We are not the first people to illuminate three primary motivators for humans. However, we've adjusted them for team learning and resiliency. We have expanded the individual mastery motivator into the essential team motivator of co-intelligence. Part One concludes by exploring the accelerator technique of organization-wide retrospectives. If you seek more examples of building high-performing teams, read Part One.

Part Two unlocks often ignored yet influential underlying challenges that affect team learning and resiliency. This includes the four most significant resilience factors: collaborative connection, embracing conflict, inclusive collaboration, and minimizing power dynamics. If you seek more examples of resilient learning teams, read Part Two.

Within each part, we present our ideas on the essential motivators and resilience factors in an order based on the peer reviewers' feedback. Each chapter was written as a stand-alone text that presents a concept for leaders to address with their teams. Yet, to achieve the full benefits, teams must exhibit all the essential motivators and resilience factors.

For each essential motivator and resilience factor, we've included stories. These stories are always based on real incidents. When we can be transparent about our direct involvement, we have listed one of our names. When we want to respect privacy, we have given fictional names.

We've included "words of advice" throughout. These tips include ideas, instructions, facilitation, and coaching techniques to get leaders heading in the right direction with the concept.

For each essential motivator and resilience factor, we've included a "But What If . . . ?" section. These questions anticipate the typical obstacles and impediments that courageous leaders experience. The answers provide tips and techniques for applying ideas in these challenging situations.

Finally, at the end of most chapters you'll find a section titled "Reflections for Learning." Use these statements to consider what you've read and to speculate about how you might apply the questions to your world.

CHAPTER 1

Break Free from Blame

Leaders want results. Too many leaders have the idea that blame or shame helps people do better. Based on research and our accumulated experience, this is not accurate.

Blame: When we blame, we censure, invalidate, or discredit others, stating or implying their professional, social, or moral irresponsibility.

Shame: When we feel shame, it's a self-conscious, self-loathing emotion. Shame promotes feelings of distress, exposure, mistrust, powerlessness, and worthlessness.

In a one-on-one session with a leader, Diana asked, "What do you want to focus on today?" The leader, Priyanka, responded, "The fact that I'm stupid." A million things were running through Diana's head, but she simply responded, "Tell me more." Priyanka talked for quite some time. She explained how she had failed at helping her team. She assumed that she wasn't knowledgeable enough. She shared that she was blamed for ineffectively communicating with the team members. She noted how exhausted she was and that there was no break in sight. She repeated that she failed the team. She kept returning to the shaming statement that she was stupid.

Diana took a step back to clarify the purpose of Priyanka's actions. She asked, "How were you trying to help? What were the outcomes you were trying to lead the team to accomplish?" Priyanka rattled them off quickly. One, her team asked her to do this. So she wanted to be responsive and helpful. Two, saving team members time by communicating on their behalf. Three, keeping everyone and everything aligned on the goal. Four, knowing the status and controlling the situation.

Then Diana asked, "With a leader being the go-between, which of these benefits would be achievable? Even with all the intelligence in the world." Priyanka paused. She raised her head just a tiny bit. She started to say, "Maybe saving . . . ," but trailed off. She interrupted herself to acknowledge, "Actually, none of these." She sighed and paused for a long, silent moment. "This approach was never going to work."

As the conversation continued, Diana heard these beautiful words: "I'm not stupid. Here's what I'm going to try next time."

Priyanka wanted to help her team, her organization, and her customers. Her intent was amazing. Her goals were what many expect from leaders. Priyanka's choice to be the go-between is not out of the ordinary. And the failure to achieve results with this approach is unsurprising. Not being a bottleneck was the issue that needed resolution. Yet their blame and her shame distracted from solving this real issue.

Faultfinding is a popular sport. It gives the illusion of making things better, but it rarely leads to real improvement. In fact, it engenders destructive emotional responses. Feeling blamed by others leads to hiding out and inaction. Fearing we'll become the target of blame leads to deflecting and hiding mistakes. Accepting the shame of "doing it wrong" decreases our sense of self-worth. Everyone on Priyanka's team, including Priyanka herself, defaulted to deciding who was at fault and why. But Priyanka was not stupid and wasn't a poor communicator. This focus created wasted energy.

When we feel blamed by others or shamed by ourselves, we cripple our ability to perform well. We become incapable of innovative, creative thought. Movement in a new direction comes with too much threat. Faultfinding, judgments, blame, and shame work together to prompt a negative downward spiral. All continue a vicious blame cycle that is unproductive. We must break free to achieve resiliency and results.

Why Breaking Free of Blame Is Critical

What do we mean by breaking free of blame? That people stop taking time to find the person to skewer with blame, including themselves. We've seen the waste and damage in business failures, as well as damage to personal and interpersonal relationships.

According to Daniel Kahneman in *Thinking Fast and Slow*, people have a propensity for substituting easier problems for hard ones.[1] Reflecting back on a problem, we may find ease in blaming people or shaming ourselves, judging people for not doing "what is common sense" or "obvious to everyone now." People don't examine the systems involved that allowed this failure to happen. Instead, they often go for the easier answer: the person should have just done their job.

In Priyanka's situation, she determined she was stupid, that she, singlehandedly, was the cause of all the problems. She publicly accepted the blame, and she privately and publicly shamed herself. As a leader, Priyanka set an example that assumes mistakes are horrible. And a mistake maker is always punished. Yet none of this actually improves the results.

If the blame and shame continued, Priyanka would be on a destructive path that could even destroy her self-confidence, abilities, and value to others. If the vicious blaming and shaming cycle continued, Priyanka would feel unsupported. She could collapse under the weight of everyone's unrealistic expectations. Then Priyanka might begin to feel victimized and to complain and justify. She might quit. Or worse, she might stay but remain in a headspace that brings herself and others down, expending energy on the target of blame and shame instead of on possible solutions. What kind of results are achievable when this is all happening?

Too many people with high potential as leaders walk away when they are stuck in this cycle, leaving individuals, teams, and organizations to suffer.

Let's examine another story.

A client assigned a task to Kevin. This task was to write an article on a team collaboration activity. Kevin understood the value of this article, so he agreed to the assignment.

Kevin struggled to write the article. He had never self-identified as a strong writer. So he delayed and delayed getting started. Finally, out loud to himself, he said, "I have to do this. I don't have a choice. Just write something." He wrote. At the next meeting, he gave it to the client. The client became confused. This article did not reflect what Kevin was capable of or what they expected. They blamed Kevin for not paying attention to the task details. They asked him to try again. So he did. Again, he delayed. Now he was in full shame mode, repeating to himself frequently how horrible he was for procrastinating, and revisiting how crazy the client was to ask him to do this.

He met with the client again. He walked into this meeting with a sense of dread. He was preparing to explain why he was horrible and feared being further judged.

Few people think, "Who can I blame today?" If you had asked the client if they forced this task on Kevin, they would have said no. It was only a request. If you had asked the client if they were judging him, they would have said no. They were giving feedback and challenging him to improve. Unfortunately, that's not what he experienced. People begin to internalize blame in the form of shame. Shame leads to lower engagement and confidence. The more Kevin disappointed his client, the more disappointed he was in himself. The more disappointed he became in himself, the more he resented the task at hand, and the worse the result became. By blaming and shaming, we pretend we can prevent the issue again. Yet each revision Kevin attempted diminished in value.

For results, leaders need to break this cycle. Breaking free from blame means embracing uncertainty and complexity. Breaking free from blame means focusing on learning and what to do next.

A development team was dependent on the marketing team to provide text for a feature in the product. Unfortunately, the marketing team had missed three sequential deadlines for providing this text. Development team members were frustrated. They complained to each other about the marketing team. They began making jokes and snarky comments.

As the leader of the team, Tricia observed repeated blaming behaviors. To get the team focused back on learning and the goal, she opened a discussion. Tricia asked the team to list reasons that marketing had missed deadlines. Answers flowed easily and were usually judgmental. Tricia then asked the team if they knew what bigger issues the marketing team might be facing. They acknowledged that they had no idea. During this conversation, one of the team members asked a valuable learning question: "We don't control the marketing team. We don't know what is really happening over there. But what can we do to help this situation?"

By ceasing to expend energy on judgment, the team discovered helpful options for both teams. Clearly, there is more to this story than one simple question. But first, we have to understand why people jump to blame and shame in the workplace.

Popular Fallacies

How did so many organizations get to a place where blame and shame regularly occur? Many organizations accept a foundation of beliefs that have wreaked havoc. In the past, these beliefs were possibly suitable for some situations. But now they have truly become outdated as they impede the achievement of results.

Fallacy: Everything can and should be more efficient. During the industrial era of organizations, businesses faced many challenges. One of the biggest was optimizing task-oriented work. Task work entails the performance of repeatable understood activities to reproduce a known output. Leadership focused on consistency and efficiency—for example, improving the speed of assembly-line work.

But not all work is task oriented. Knowledge work entails having a rough idea of the goal upfront, then working together to discover value. This means constant learning, unclear activities, and new, evolving outputs.

Knowledge work requires different leadership and processes. Thus, when leaders try to manage knowledge work as task work, blame and shame increase. The goal of being efficient (fast) before being effective (valuable) forges a losing strategy—for example, asking people for yearlong detailed estimates on knowledge work (crazy!), then blaming people for missing estimates that were always only guesses (even crazier!).

Acclaimed management thinker Peter Drucker wrote, "The most valuable asset of a 21st-century institution will be its knowledge workers." Drucker described a "knowledge worker" in 1966 (The Effective Executive) as an employee who thinks, using cognitive rather than physical abilities.[2]

Fallacy: Everything hinges on shareholder value and profitability. When the balance of attention goes to increasing shareholder value, stakeholders suffer. Stakeholders include employees, customers, vendors, and the surrounding community. A focus on shareholder value intensifies the problem of prioritizing efficiencies over effectiveness. Organizations focus on quarterly profitability rather than longer-term, sustainable performance. Businesses tend to manage by driving down costs to show bottom-line savings for each quarter. They miss opportunities for growing the top line to increase revenue. When cuts become untenable, blame increases—blaming employee productivity, blaming vendors for pricing, blaming customers for not knowing up front exactly what they need. This drives knowledge workers to urgent, short-term productivity. This short-term approach benefits only shareholders. Ultimately, both shareholders and stakeholders lose.[3]

Fallacy: Everything is a "project." Traditionally project success is defined by three goals: meets requirements; under budget; and on time. Nowhere in this definition is customer satisfaction. The definition assumes the output is completely known (task work). If that is true, then "meets requirements" assumes customer satisfaction. But this definition fails with knowledge work. The reality is that often stakeholders don't know what they don't know about what they need. Value discovery comes from cycles of feedback. Attention to product delivery produces more effectiveness than a focus on project success. Yet many organizational processes center on projects, not products. Thus, blaming occurs—blaming stakeholders who changed their minds, blaming employees for not asking the right questions, blame that work doesn't fit into the financial accounting structures.[4]

Fallacy: Every leader must have all the answers. There are many reasons for leadership role promotions. Three common ones are time in role, individual expertise, and problem-solving ability. In task work, leadership had all the answers due to previous experience. The command-and-control style of leadership is sufficiently effective for task work. Yet in knowledge work, when leaders don't have the answers, they become the target of blame and shame. When teams don't meet their goals, leaders blame employees, and employees blame leaders for having unrealistic expectations. In knowledge work, leaders cannot control and guarantee results. No one can. Nor will one person ever have all the answers. Leaders want knowledge workers closest to the outcomes to achieve the goal together.[5]

Learning Leaders 4Cs

Learning leaders support leaders at all levels to become learning leaders too. They build resiliency from outside and inside the team.

They build resiliency with the key elements that increase the odds of success. Chip Bell, in "Great Leaders Learn Out Loud," exhorted leaders to "learn out loud."[6] We find "learning out loud" makes a difference. To show a commitment to learning, learning leaders embrace, model, and activate four elements: courage, compassion, confidence, and complexity (the Learning Leaders 4Cs; Figure 1.1).

Courage

Courage showcases the favorable behaviors we want to reveal in teams. To show courage, leaders stand up for learning, their own and others'. Learning leaders advocate for team, organization, and individual learning time. They show curiosity about discovering what's needed for the next deliverable. They share their willingness to explore their vulnerabilities and ask for help.

Compassion

Compassion encourages valuable concern and interactions during challenges and failures. With a compassionate approach, the

Figure 1.1 Learning Leaders 4Cs

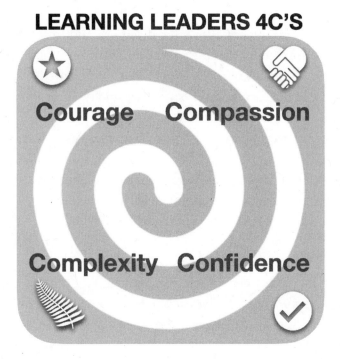

leader recognizes the difficulties of learning for anyone. They understand that developing new skills takes time, and it may even negatively affect short-term production. They respect that people, including themselves, may have leftover fears about learning. They provide a safety net for learning.

Confidence

Confidence develops in a team's ability to learn whatever they need to meet the challenge. With confidence, growth in professional skills and interaction behaviors emerges. The learning leader's confidence expands along with the team's ability to move ahead. Simply put, they believe in others.

Complexity

Complexity awareness allows for discovery and unleashing the power of emergent valuable solutions. With complexity awareness, critical thinking behaviors take on renewed emphasis. Learning leaders act from a systemic viewpoint. They look for the systemic roots of problems. They understand that more actionable information surfaces as the team continues to learn.[7]

Before a half-day sales team reflection meeting, Tricia was finishing preparations. As each participant arrived, they approached Tricia with similar cautions: "John is not going to like this." "John doesn't do activities." "John will probably not participate." Her response to each warning was, "I have confidence in this team's ability to work together." As he was the only one who didn't approach her, she knew who John was immediately.

Tricia became a little more nervous with each successive warning. Yet she had taken several things into consideration that she knew would help John and others. Tricia had considered how to enable learning and foster a collaborative tone. As a result, she let the nerves go and felt confident that John would be able to contribute.

As the meeting began, the anxiety in the room was noticeable. Teammates wondered what John would or wouldn't do. During the first major activity, Tricia invited people to shout out their opinions. She noticed John hesitated to share his thoughts. She acknowledged that learning can be challenging, as we have to slow down to speed up. Then she instructed everyone to discuss the topic in pairs. The pair would decide who would share its opinion with the larger group. Tricia observed John engaging with his partner. When it came time to share, John's partner shared John's opinion. The room acknowledged each opinion. Tricia reinforced the importance of hearing various opinions. She noted that the variety would be valuable for the team in determining how to proceed on a new solution. Throughout the rest of the meeting, John continued to engage in each activity.

At the end, John approached Tricia. In front of the team, he said, "I usually don't like these things, but somehow I liked today. I don't know how I feel about you." Then he walked away with a smile on his face. This remains one of the best compliments Tricia ever received.

It is important to note that John was not difficult for the sake of being difficult. He did not enjoy any large room full of people shouting over each other. He did not enjoy meetings that never seemed to get results. Who does? The difference is that John showed courage by not playing along. We respect this response. There will never be a single perfect design for all situations.

The 4Cs create spaces for people to thrive and contribute together. Learning leaders continuously and courageously embody these four elements. By reassuring team members that things would be OK, Tricia demonstrated her confidence in their team's ability to figure it out. By adjusting the activity to pairs, she showed compassion for engagement challenges. By expressing the importance of hearing all voices, Tricia showcased the behaviors desired. By noting the value of variety, she brought complexity awareness to the tasks at hand. As a result, John was able to fully engage, collaborate, and learn with the team. The team benefited from his contributions. Together, they realized that all their perspectives made better solutions.

With behaviors that support the 4Cs, learning leaders foster the right environment.

Introduction to Leadership through Learning

Breaking free from blame, learning leaders begin a journey into leadership through learning (Figure 1.2).

Figure 1.2 Leadership through Learning

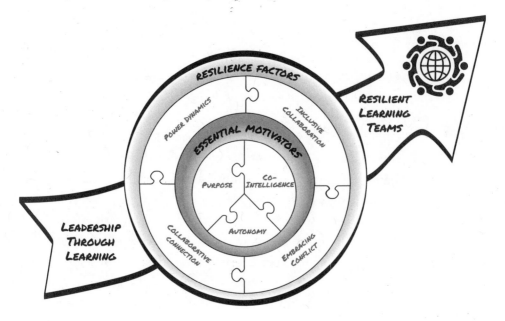

Leadership through learning reflects the leader's role in growing team resilience to discover lasting value. Learning leaders build resilient learning teams. Resilience is the human ability to meet and recover from adversity and setbacks. We need learning across the board; for leaders, for our teams, and for our organizations.

Resilient learning teams have the ability to sustain under pressure and chaos. They overcome major difficulties without engaging in dysfunctional behavior or harming others. A resilient learning team provides a foundation for enabling business agility.

The high degree of uncertainty in this world leads to the need for flexibility and resiliency—the ability to bounce back from adverse events. As chaos unfolds, it requires people to collaborate and learn together. In a VUCA world, "speed to learning" becomes a crucial indicator for enabling business agility.

Business Agility

Business agility is the ability of an organization to sense changes internally or externally and respond accordingly in order to deliver value to its customers.

Business agility is not a specific methodology or even a general framework. It's a description of how an organization operates by embodying a specific type of growth mindset that is very similar to the agile mindset often described by members of the agile software development community. It's appropriate for any organization that faces uncertainty and rapid change.[8]

Our use of the term VUCA comes from the article in *Harvard Business Review* by Nathan Bennett and G. James Lemoine.[9] In it, the authors introduced the acronym into the business world. Coined by the US Army War College, VUCA was intended to capture a set of characteristics. It stands for "volatile, uncertain, complex, and ambiguous." It described the conditions squads of soldiers encountered after deployment on a mission. Following plans made at headquarters cost lives. HQ officers could not take into account the rapidly changing situations these squads found in the field. Army trainers acknowledged that these conditions altered assumptions about the chain of command. Soldiers needed new skills, understanding, and mindsets. Training with VUCA allowed them to react and respond to the scene they discovered. For resilience in business, as well as warfare, leaders need to equip themselves differently. Both officers and business leaders need to rethink their skills, their approaches, and their thinking about leadership.

All teams face, or will face, VUCA barriers to success. Leadership through learning encourages and enables whole team learning. A learning leader embraces complexity awareness and aids the team in learning how to overcome barriers together. Peter

Senge coined the term *learning organization,* defining it as "a team of people working together collectively to enhance their capacities to create results they really care about."[10] Learning leaders create evolving learning organizations that minimize blame and shame. When people collaborate and learn together, they focus less on individual success or failures.

Business agility is a multifaceted topic for every organization. This book focuses solely on leadership's ability to set up teams to be effective and resilient, thus providing organizations the team capabilities needed to achieve any business agility strategies.

We cannot provide one simple, comprehensive checklist for achieving leadership through learning. The challenge holds more nuance and situational variety than that. Yet leaders will find value in discovering essential motivators and resilience factors for building team resilience.

In Part One, we describe three essential motivators for teams. They lay the foundation for enabling high performance. We are not the first to illuminate three primary motivators for humans. But we've adjusted the concept for team learning and resiliency. We have expanded the mastery motivator into the essential team motivator of co-intelligence. Essential motivators help expand confidence, as the team shares responsibility for results. Besides, learning leaders understand that team resiliency is not automatic; it must be proactively and compassionately addressed.

In Part Two, the resilience factors take the team further. The resilience factors are collaborative connections, inclusive collaboration, power dynamics, and embracing conflict. These factors compose the "secret sauce" or the "underlying forces" for building resilience. These either courageously evolve teams or break teams in times of chaos.

Reflections for Your Learning

Begin your journey of breaking free from blame and shame today. Learning leaders focus intensely on resilient learning for the organization, teams, and themselves.

How does blame or shame manifest in your organization?

How would breaking free from blame create benefits in your organization?

Which leadership fallacies are present in your organization? Why? What is the impact?

How has learning influenced your leadership behavior? How have you supported others' learning?

How do you embody the Learning Leaders 4Cs in your leadership?

The Essential Motivators

I n Part One, we introduce the *essential motivators*.

Leadership through learning respects the resiliency needed to discover value. We must learn across the board; for leaders, for our teams, and for our organizations. For an optimal learning environment, learning leaders focus on the motivation of others.

According to Daniel Pink, author of *Drive*, motivating knowledge workers requires new approaches.[1] Approaches such as innovation bonuses do not produce optimal results. Instead, he highlights the essential motivators of purpose, mastery, and autonomy. These three lay the foundation for enabling high performance individually. With the focus of team high performance, **purpose** and **autonomy** remain essential motivators. We have expanded the individual mastery motivator into the essential motivator of **co-intelligence**. These essential motivators help the team share responsibility for results.[2]

In the following four chapters, we'll explore the three essential motivators. You can read them in any order, but learning leaders will need them all. In Chapter 2, we'll examine the shift in leadership for these essential motivators. We'll discuss the importance of shared responsibility to increase team autonomy. In Chapter 3, we'll explain the benefits of alignment. We'll explore why there is a growing need for a motivating, meaningful purpose for resiliency. In Chapter 4, we'll analyze the importance of continuous learning. We'll discover why developing co-intelligence is as important as competency within teams. In Chapter 5, we'll examine a retrospective example on accelerating the essential motivators.

CHAPTER 2

The Shift toward Leading Resilient Learning Teams

Leaders tend to lead the way that others led them. Unfortunately, not all past or present leaders deserve emulation.

As Peter Drucker, a renowned management expert, said, "So much of what we call management consists in making it difficult for people to work."[1] These management behaviors come out of habit or procedure, not necessarily by intention. Not all managers act as leaders. Not all leaders have manager roles.

Ideally, people with management titles act as both managers and leaders. When they don't, the negative impact is great. Data published in Development Dimensions International's Frontline Leader Project indicates that 57 percent of employees have left a job because of their manager. An additional 32 percent have seriously considered leaving because of their manager.[2] Yet we continue to hear business quotes that perpetuate harm (Figure 2.1).

Many leaders and managers have stated this sentiment. It is from a movie, *The Godfather* (1972), based on a fictional crime family.[3] People quote a fictional mob boss as a role model for their leadership perspective. The good intention is to assert that a decision was not made out of a desire to hurt the person. But when people use this quote, they are only comforting themselves.

For example, take terminations based on a performance issue like lateness. It may seem objectively appropriate. But when we

Figure 2.1 Dangerous Leadership Quote One

look further, we may discover more things that need to be taken into consideration. That valuable employee may have experienced difficulties, such as the illness of someone close. As a result, the employee is juggling a lot of new responsibilities outside work. Unfortunately, they didn't trust their leader enough to confide in them. After being fired, the employee must figure out how they will feed their family and get a new job. The "objectively driven" termination carries very personal impacts for them. As for the leader, they now must invest money in replacing this knowledgeable employee. The leader may have to handle long-term repercussions, such as the grapevine working overtime—others may hear about the termination, take sides, and become increasingly distrustful. This results in people feeling like cogs in the machine and trust being broken. This establishes a suboptimal environment for achieving results.

Figure 2.2 Dangerous Leadership Quote Two

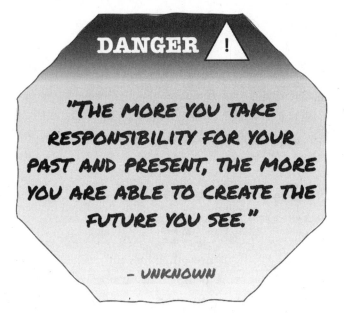

Or how about the perspective in Figure 2.2?

We've heard this from leaders who want to focus on past mistakes. This might seem to be a solid leadership concept. The trick lies in discerning what the quote means by "responsibility." The danger is if the focus on past errors comes with judgment as an attempt to prevent future mistakes. There is too much complexity to ever guarantee the future.

As work shifts to more knowledge work, leadership needs to shift as well. We advocate that leaders become learning leaders. Instead of "Why did you make this mistake?" shift to "What can we learn together now?"

Blame and Accountability

People engage in misguided attempts to guarantee results. The goal, "I'm going to hold Lee accountable for completing the task," makes it too easy to point fingers. What does that mean?

Task: A commitment or expectation to perform an action that may be imposed or selected.
Accountability: An expectation to provide and report information about the work progress and quality.

By definition, this statement demands that someone report information on a task status. Lee may not even be the one doing the task. Yet we've seen the "hold them accountable" endeavor as an attempt to guarantee tasks' completion. In task-based work, reports are a more or less accurate representation of progress. However, in knowledge work, this approach fails.

Discovery of value is essential in knowledge work. It entails many unknowns that people can't plan for or control. Knowledge-based tasks may not meet the original estimates—at no fault of the employee. In these cases, leaders waste time and energy when they focus on blaming. Mistakes or errors in judgment are rarely intentional.

Blaming as a means to control future behaviors and results is a legacy. It's a relic from predictable task-based work and industrial thinking. It has no place in an ever-changing, knowledge work world. Blame arises from expecting controllability for tasks that are uncertain and unpredictable. Shame arises from imposing expectations where the task may have been impossible.

That said, accountability, the act of reporting, plays an important role. Reporting acts as a stimulus for transparency and communication. But learning leaders do not treat accountability as a means to force unrealistic guarantees.

I need support, encouragement, and accountability.
I need to be a member of a community to do my
best. A key to performing well is accountability:
making commitments, working in ways I am proud of,
and rendering account of my activities clearly and
directly. . . . Accountability can be offered, asked, even
demanded, but it cannot be forced. — Kent Beck[4]

Instead, leaders shift their emphasis. Keep the focus on learning, not blaming.

Leaders' Impact on Blame

We've never seen leaders sitting around a table asking, "How can we make everyone else miserable today?" Most leaders have good intentions. But they may fail to realize the mixed messages they send to the team that lead to blame and shame.

Juan was puzzled with his team's lack of willingness to experiment. He kept telling them that there would be no punishment for failing. He kept asking what the team wanted to try next. All to no avail. Finally, one day Juan asked a senior member of the team directly, "What am I missing? What is everyone afraid of?" The senior member said, "You never fail. We don't want to let you down."

Juan was shocked. He failed all the time. He was constantly experimenting and learning. But he had not shared his failures and learnings with the team.

Juan's team respected him as a leader. He was trying to be a learning leader and wasn't blaming others for not experimenting.

But he forgot to be courageously transparent about his own learning. Instead, his perceived excellence led others to feel that the bar was too high. This accidental mixed message led the team to be afraid and to want to avoid the shame of letting him down. So they avoided risk. In doing so, they also avoided getting amazing results.

> *Angie, a project manager, was trying to get status updates for the big fund-raising event at the end of the month. She got tired of trying to track down each person. Instead, she held a meeting and invited everyone. During this meeting, Angie asked each person for their updates. At one point, everyone realized that no one had contacted a key vendor. It was a huge oversight that could force them to cancel the event. For the next hour, debates and accusations flew around the room. People blamed others, both in and out of the meeting.*

Angie contributed to creating an environment where self-protection became the first priority. By having people report status to her, she didn't show confidence in her team's ability to work together. By being the single point of information, Angie reinforced that they were individual contributors. Her behavior implied that she was accountable for making sure nothing was missed. So when the team realized the mistake, there was concern about whom Angie would blame.

When she held a single meeting to bring them together, Angie was trying to be a learning leader. She accepted that she couldn't handle everything. She was aware of the complexity that many things contributed to this oversight. Was this oversight even avoidable? What systemic factors contributed to it? As Angie observed the blaming, she realized the problem still remained. She knew she had to focus the team on learning and working together.

Laura celebrated her recent hire as a new customer support manager. She enjoys working with her team. Yet she struggles with her manager—specifically regarding conflicting stakeholder priorities. When Laura raised this issue with her manager, his initial reaction was, "This is just how it is here."

Laura began searching for better ideas about how to manage up. Unfortunately, every attempt by Laura to get her manager on board failed. In fact, the conflicting priorities seemed to be getting worse. Suddenly, Laura found herself resentful. She began ignoring issues, including the team mocking senior management.

Stephen Covey, in *The 7 Habits of Highly Effective People*, notes that the more people focus on areas outside their control, the less they can influence change.[5] Conflicting priorities affected Laura's team. Yet Laura did not have authority over the situation. The more her frustration grew over the lack of resolution, the more trust broke. As she attempted to "manage up," her behaviors had a tone of blame. This didn't create energy toward finding a solution. Instead, her manager put energy into self-protection.

Laura may not have had enough control over the situation to fix the issue. However, she did have control over how she approached it. She had control over how she reacted and communicated. She had control over how she focused the team. In being a learning leader, she compassionately explored what her manager might be enduring. This unlocked ideas for how Laura could contribute to creating valuable interactions.

Responsibility

People may expect that leaders are also experts. They expect them to know everything, to make sure everything happens. The "expert leader" assumption means the leader becomes the constriction point to progress. In other words, the leader becomes the bottle-neck. Outcomes only scale to that single individual's capability and capacity. Welcome to the world of 70-plus-hour workweeks for managers. What an unreasonable burden to carry when help is all around!

To start, learning leaders must *invite* responsibility to achieve results.

Responsibility: "I have the power and the ability to find and resolve the real problem." When I have the responsibility mindset that this is mine to solve or to act on, I can access new options to make changes.[6]

Responsibility comes from inside; it's a feeling of being willing to take ownership. Learning leaders focus on creating shared responsibility for team results. When people experience shared responsibility, their investment and results skyrocket. Thus, team members willingly hold themselves accountable to transparently acknowledging the situation.

Obligation: An obligation is a mandatory course of action regardless of control or interest.
   "I have to do this. I have no choice."

Responsibility is different from obligation. When people feel they have no control, they don't deliver their best work. From Chapter 1, remember the story about Kevin writing an article on a team collaboration activity. He felt obligation, not responsibility. As a result, he wasn't open about his insecurities. Without that transparency, blame and shame took over, creating a disappointing outcome. Choosing responsibility has a dramatic impact on achieving results.

> *After another round of disappointing results, the client changed the approach. Instead of blaming Kevin for the lackluster outcome, he asked, "Do you want to write this article?" Kevin realized that he had never asked himself this, nor had he been asked by others. He paused to think. At that moment, he knew he was in full, pressured obligation mode. Continuing to remain in the "I have to . . ." stance was not helping anyone. He had to make a choice either to take responsibility for writing the article or to not write it.*
>
> *Kevin chose to write the article. But first, he knew he had to openly discuss his fears. This discussion helped him find ways to approach writing differently. On subsequent drafts, his negative self-talk quieted. The next meeting review had a completely different outcome. His client expressed his pleasant surprise at the changes. After some minor edits, the article was published.*

The client's shift toward inviting Kevin to affirm his choice made the difference. Once Kevin felt responsible, his interest, openness, passion, and creativity took off. By fostering responsibility, teams propel action forward. Responsibility embraces acknowledging and admitting the truth without judgment. Everyone acknowledges their mistakes. Everyone acknowledges their role in unwanted outcomes. Everyone acknowledges the reality of the situation. Responsibility with acknowledgment focuses everyone on a learning opportunity together.

Team over Individuals

In knowledge work, learning leaders need teams that share responsibility.

As described by Etsy CTO John Allspaw in a blog post, "People at Etsy who mess up are given the opportunity to give a detailed account of what they did, the effects they had, their expectations and assumptions, and what they think happened *without fear of punishment*."[7]

Etsy also gives out an annual award—a real three-armed sweater—to an employee who's made an error. The award clearly shows that at Etsy, accidents are seen as a valuable source of data. They aren't regarded as something embarrassing to shy away from. The sweater goes to whomever made the most surprising error. Not the worst one—the most unexpected one. The award serves as a reminder to always be willing to learn.

Teams work on deliverables intended to benefit the business. Team compositions of diverse skills, backgrounds, years of experience, cognitive tendencies, and more will add flexibility, versatility, and resilience to the organization's ability to deliver. Yet labeling a team of people a "team" does not mean they function as a team. Let's unpack the differences in team evolution (Figure 2.3).

Individuals focus on independent work with little need to coordinate with others. People are primarily worried about themselves, their skill sets, and their individual performance. For task-based work, individual contributors are often successful.

Groups focus on coordinating and cooperating to complete distinct parts of the work. In this state, work is like a relay race. This means one shared goal, with each person having a discrete part. Cooperation sounds like, "I'll help you with what you need to do, once mine is done." This can lead to deeming discrete parts successful even if the common goal is unmet. For task-based work, a team can achieve high performance.

Teams focus on collaborating together to complete a common goal. Collaboration is "our part," not the cooperation of "your

Figure 2.3 Resilient Learning Team Evolution

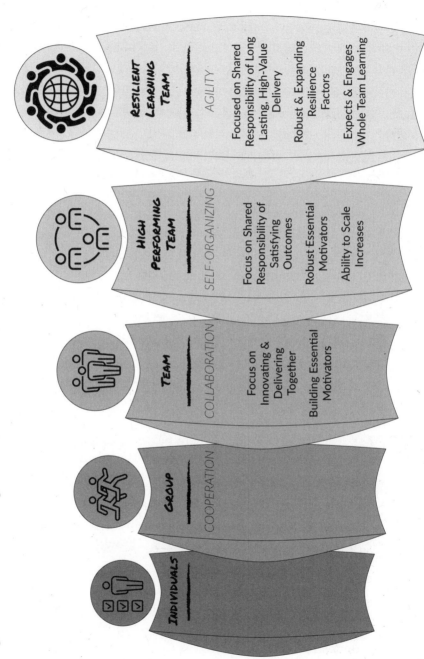

part, my part." In this state, team members are working well together to discover ways to meet the common goal. Yet the leader
is still the focal point of the team. Being a go-between might have
been necessary to help get the team to this state. But eventually
this approach creates a bottleneck, preventing the team from
achieving the next level of performance. With knowledge-based
work, leaders need at least a team to begin to discover value.

High-performance teams are collaborating, self-organizing
units that have shared responsibility for satisfying outcomes.
This means jointly determining how team members complete the
work, based on the synergy of their combined strengths, skills,
and interests. The leader is no longer the focal point, which enables the scaling of results. These characteristics are consistently
present within the entire team:

- work collaboratively and gain synergy
- problem solve the workflows and systems
- exhibit strong cohesiveness
- increase collective productivity and accountability
- share informal leadership
- reflect outcome improvement
- seek training and mentoring to build capabilities
- strive to create psychological safety
- take risks for innovation
- be willing to show incomplete work, express failures,
  explore alternatives, and raise impediments
- embrace conflict as opportunities for growth and
  understanding

Resilient learning teams build on high-performance teams.
Resilient learning teams thrive and produce in high uncertainty.
They emphasize shared responsibility to respond to emergent con-

ditions. They enable business agility by anticipating and responding to changing realities. They embody the essence of agility. Resilient learning teams exhibit the characteristics of high-performance teams, as well as the following:

- show resilience to setbacks and quickly learn from perceived failures
- amplify the value of learning together
- anticipate future business and customer needs
- welcome and celebrate complex problems
- consistently build connections for trust to challenge themselves and others
- expect greater psychological safety
- proactively increase their diversity and inclusion
- manage power relationships for greater effectiveness
- pursue conflict as a path to creativity and innovation

Resilient learning teams get right to the business of working through chaos together. They take action, then assess the results of the action and learn from them. Those findings inform their next collective action. This learning prepares them for the next chaos, which will inevitably arise. Resilient learning teams move through chaos to the complexity on the other side. They assume that any lulls in the chaos are only temporary, and that together they will learn and succeed.

Building Autonomy

A resilient learning team emphasizes shared responsibility to respond to emergent conditions (Figure 2.4).

To build shared responsibility with and within the team, increase team autonomy. When we feel empowered to make

Figure 2.4 Leadership through Learning

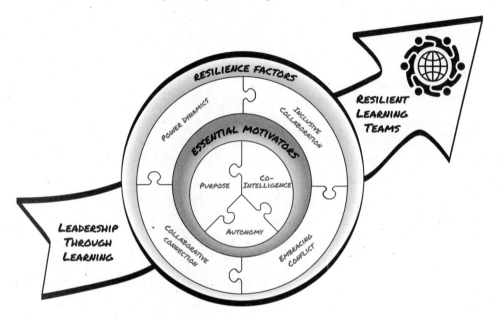

decisions, we experience autonomy. Our sense of autonomy implies the recognition that we exercise appropriate control over our work—how we do it, when we do it, and whom we do it with.

Team autonomy requires a supportive environment. It's not enough to communicate, "You're empowered," then walk away.

Diana consulted with an organization that sought the benefits of agility. Together, they identified areas of work that would serve as the pilots for change. Employees accepted an invitation to choose which team they would join. The consulting team worked with managers to create a plan for investing in team learning.

Quickly, in the new way of working, the teams hit a roadblock. Most of their managers reacted in one of two ways. Either they became apprehensive that the teams wouldn't get the work done and began micromanaging, or they abstained from assuming any responsibility. They said, "You're a team now. We've empowered you. You've had training." In both cases, the team lost trust in their managers.

Managers lacked the capability to provide an environment for teamwork. They didn't understand their role as stewards of the new way of working. They didn't understand how to support and progressively enable the teams. They didn't help the teams take more control over their work. Managers didn't know how to create a work environment where the team members felt safe to make decisions. Consequently, team members found little opportunity to develop autonomy. And the teams struggled to produce results. It became clear that the managers needed training, coaching, and mentoring too.

Don't worry: the story ended well. The pilot teams succeeded. Senior leaders recognized their omission. They had dived into investing in team learning before helping the managers learn. The good news came when everyone realized it wasn't too late to catch up. With support for their learning, managers gained skills in becoming learning leaders. They even formed their own cohort for learning going forward.

You can't demand change. People must feel safe to take responsibility and autonomy for their actions.

Researchers have produced several models of what psychological safety encompasses. Each model highlights various triggers that hinder learning, collaboration, and performance. A consistent finding is that blame and shame contribute to triggers for undermining psychological safety. To measure a team's level of psychological safety, Edmondson asked how strongly team members agreed or disagreed with these statements:[8]

Psychological safety is being able to show and employ oneself without fear of negative consequences of self-image, status, or career.[9]

Edgar H. Schein and Warren Bennis first introduced the term "psychological safety" as a catalyst for organizational change. Schein and Bennis built on Lewin's three-stage model of organizational learning and change by suggesting that psychologically safe work environments facilitate the "unfreezing" process where employees become perceptive to changes to the status quo.[10]

Amy Edmondson first introduced the concept of "team psychological safety": a shared belief held by members of a team that the team is safe for interpersonal risk taking.[11]

Timothy R. Clark contributed to the concept of psychological safety with the 4 Stages of Psychological Safety framework. He defines psychological safety as "a condition in which human beings feel (1) included, (2) safe to learn, (3) safe to contribute, and (4) safe to challenge the status quo—all without fear of being embarrassed, marginalized, or punished in some way."[12]

- If you make a mistake on this team, it is often held against you.
- Members of this team are able to bring up problems and tough issues.
- People on this team sometimes reject others for being different.
- It is safe to take a risk on this team.
- It is difficult to ask other members of this team for help.
- No one on this team would deliberately act in a way that undermines my efforts.
- Working with members of this team, my unique skills and talents are valued and utilized.

As each person has their own experiences, leaders cannot avoid safety triggers 100 percent. Yet learning leaders can lessen and mitigate triggers and their impacts. Build psychological safety and team autonomy by doing the following:

1. **Invest in team learning.** It's folly to expect people to do something they don't know how to do. Provide support, encouragement, and compassion about the learning journey. And create environments where the team learns together. Learning can happen in many approaches. Classroom training isn't the only answer. Explore the Agile Fluency Model to find ideas for investment.[13] Consider mentoring between team members. Try working in small groups to support learning by osmosis and proximity. Support learning hours for specific work-related interests. Support brown-bag lunches for team members to share what they've learned with others.

2. **Provide boundaries or guard rails.** Respect complexity by keeping the boundaries around the work clear and focused. Ensure the boundaries are not so narrow that the team is completely dependent on the leader. But also check to make sure the initial boundaries aren't so broad that they encourage "boiling the ocean." Continue to expand the boundaries over time in response to the teams' requests and growth.

3. **Expect discoveries.** In knowledge work, the practice of identifying the needs in advance is no longer viable. New information constantly emerges as learning problems to solve. By acknowledging this, we honor complexity. Keep having the team ask questions. The more autonomy they feel, the more responsibility they will take for the outcomes, even with the unexpected.

4. **Demonstrate courage, patience, and confidence.** It is
   important for leaders to courageously share their own
   learning interests and paths as leaders. This requires
   vulnerability but builds trust. It also highlights that
   the most powerful ability leaders can supply is
   patience—for themselves and for others. Learning
   curves are real. We slow down at first to speed up later.
   Reassure your colleagues that you understand the need
   for continuous learning. Show you have confidence in
   the team's capability and approach.

Leadership through learning involves making shifts in attitude and behavior. It means moving away from the idea that
blame is a motivator. It means embracing new ways of introducing responsibility. It means thinking in terms of teams and systems rather than individual effort. Leaders shift their perspective
to achieving outcomes and impacts rather than achieving discrete tasks.

Learning leaders courageously accept that team autonomy
contributes to success—and in better ways than outdated management techniques. They understand that team autonomy
doesn't happen by closing people in a room and locking the
door. They compassionately support team growth toward autonomy. They embrace the complexity reflected by team requests
for responsibility and decision making. And they show confidence
in the team's ability to learn and move forward together to any
realigned goals.

But What If . . . ?

- *No one will be responsible and nothing gets done?*
  We have never met a person who told us, "I'm planning
  to do a terrible job today." Doing a good job and solving

problems motivates people. If your organization has disengaged people, they are rarely just bad humans. Instead, this is often a symptom of leadership and organizational failures. It is also important not to rewrite history. How many dates have you missed? How has the blame game been working?

- *I'm accountable to make sure my team doesn't fail?* Leaders may feel personally accountable or have experience of this expectation. Leaders tend to hold on to existing, familiar approaches, even when these approaches are no longer serving their original purpose. When leaders prioritize short-term reactions over building resilient learning teams, everyone suffers. The leader feels overwhelmed and frustrated that the teams are not stepping up. The teams feel a lack of responsibility and fear of failing. No one is winning, especially your customer. Failures create learning opportunities that strengthen team skills long term. And learning leaders build skills in how to communicate their leadership approach. They don't give in to others' unrealistic or damaging expectations; they protect their teams from them.

- *The team won't move on from previous blaming experiences?* If people have suffered in blame and shame, there will be lasting impacts, including fear. That fear doesn't disappear because leaders stopped blaming for two weeks. Psychological safety requires repairing and rebuilding both ways. Take time to be radically transparent about the previous experiences and the impacts. Listen to the fears and concerns people need to share. Take responsibility for any part that you contributed to. Ask for ways to receive feedback if old habits return.

- *Senior leadership wants to continue to blame, and they want names?*

  Do they really want this? If they do, help educate. Leaders don't know what they don't know. They lead from their experiences, which are often of task-based work. This is the long-overdue shift needed. But as you embark on this shift, you will have to bring others with you. Help them see alternative valuable ways. Leaders want to achieve results, so help them.

Reflections for Your Learning

Begin your shift in leadership today. Learning leaders focus intensely on resilient learning for the organization, teams, and themselves.

How does your blame or shame manifest in your organization?

How have you influenced blame and shame in your organization?

How are you impeding the team's ability to choose responsibility?

How are you encouraging team collaboration?

How do you nurture team members' autonomy in their work lives, challenges, and workflow?

How do the Learning Leaders 4Cs (compassion, complexity, confidence, and courage) affect autonomy?

CHAPTER 3

The Benefits of Alignment

As learning leaders increase autonomy, they also help teams continue to work together. Too often, people focus on what needs completion while ignoring the "why." Yet an alignment with the why of their work provides extra motivation and creativity. Every employee and every team needs a sense of purpose. They want to understand the impact they have on their customers.

A human resources (HR) team was quickly burning out. When asked, they said they had no idea about how they fit into the business strategy. And they complained that they had no choice about their workload.

A learning leader, Joel realized the team was drowning in obligation. He knew the team had autonomy. But they seemed to be unable to prioritize and constantly revisit decisions. He wondered how he could help the team take responsibility.

He led a meeting to uncover and align on the purpose the HR team served in the organization. They determined that having great recruiting and hiring processes ensured a capable workforce. They defined a vision for their work as, "Our company's customers choose our products because we innovate. We innovate because we ensure our employees have the best work environment." From this vision, they described all the work of the team and how it connected to the vision. Now the team understood their role in getting the best people and giving them the best workplace, as well as how that work helped the organization prosper.

Purpose is an essential motivator for building alignment in teams. A purpose has to be big enough that all contributing parties have a role for mutual success. A clear team purpose requires that everyone is on board, and success is all or none. No single team member can be successful in achieving this purpose without the whole team. Otherwise, team members may struggle to collaborate.

Purpose is an essential motivator for all kinds of teams, including leadership teams. We're promoting the idea of learning leaders. Let's examine the purpose of leadership through learning by discussing the external, internal, and individual benefits.

External Business Benefits

Organizations gain long-lasting business success from focusing on customer satisfaction.

For high customer satisfaction, the ability to produce high-value delivery is paramount. Resilient learning teams continuously discover and deliver what customers want and need. Customers accept the product and services. They exchange value that creates benefits for the business. Team members can easily maintain and support the deliverables. Further, the environment leaves team members ready and eager to work on the next deliverable.

In a fast-changing business situation with new technologies, "strategy is simply the development of the organization's ability to learn. The organization's ability to learn faster (and possibly

> According to Peter F. Drucker, "Customers are the foundation of a business and keep it in existence. . . . Because its purpose is to create a customer, the business enterprise has two—and only these two—basic functions: Marketing and innovation produce results; all the rest are costs."[1]

better) than the competition becomes its most sustainable competitive advantage," says Arie de Gues in *The Living Company*.[2] Rarely is any problem, situation, or outcome exactly the same as those that came before. We must embrace relentless change. High-performing teams embrace discovering value to produce high-value delivery. Resilient learning teams produce high-value delivery even when chaos unfolds all around.

Internal Business Benefits

Organizations cannot survive without customers. And organizations are only as good as the people within them. To achieve long-lasting success, learning leaders design environments that foster engagement toward high-value delivery.

Gallup's *State of the Global Workplace* 2021 states that engaged employees are highly involved in and enthusiastic about their work and workplace.[3] Engaged employees significantly outperform the disengaged. They drive performance and innovation, and they move the organization forward, whereas disengaged employees disconnect at work. They may even be resentful that their needs are not met. They may consciously or unconsciously sabotage effort or momentum. Disengaged employees may act out by undermining the accomplishments of their engaged coworkers.

Employee engagement reflects the involvement and enthusiasm of employees in their work and workplace. Business units with high employee engagement achieve higher productivity, higher customer loyalty/engagement, better safety, lower turnover and higher profitability, among other positive business outcomes, according to a Gallup study of more than 100,000 business units.

Unfortunately, Gallup research also found only 34 percent for the United States and Canada and 20 percent globally.[4]

Leaders can perform a quick, subjective assessment of employee engagement. Set aside time to observe whether the following statements are true:

- Teams produce high-value delivery frequently.
- The high-value delivery outperforms in the marketplace.
- Team members report being fully immersed in and energized about their work.
- Everyone maintains a positive attitude toward the organization, their colleagues, and customers.
- Any employee becomes an advocate for their organization's reputation and interests.
- The environment reduces turnover and costs.

We see changed dynamics in workplaces where learning and engagement are at the core. People balance their work, social, and family time. They find rewards in all three. They say things like, "I feel like our work makes a difference"; "I enjoy the things I learn from the other team members. It's made me a better professional"; "I can rely on everyone to do their best, and that makes me want to bring my best self to work too"; "I want to succeed in my role because I can see how our products help our customers."

Engaged employees form into teams that reach for high performance. High-performing teams discover and produce high-value delivery. High-value delivery means customer success. Resilient learning teams take responsibility for achieving customer success even in chaos. None of these are possible without learning leaders fostering engagement.

Leader Benefits

The path to becoming a learning leader motivates everyone to go further.

Learning leaders see how the outcomes of their work affect their teams. They find new rewards in helping others level up, helping team members find confidence, helping people tackle a tough assignment, helping people feel supported when they are struggling, and helping people discover satisfying work and learn they can be good at it—for example, offering a new area of responsibility; ensuring the necessary equipment, information, and budget are in place; then supporting the team as they step up to the responsibility in ways you, and they, didn't expect. It is exciting to see them grow their own belief in themselves and to feel that confidence in the team.

Learning leaders see how outcomes of the team's work affect their stakeholders. For example, a leader sponsored a team field trip. The team of technicians assembled probes for use with mass spectrometers (used in analyzing chemical samples). The team visited a hospital lab where the lab specialists showed the probes in use. Then they talked with a recovering patient. He thanked them for the quality and accuracy of the equipment. It turned out that the patient's diagnosis depended on the precise data the probes provided. "Your tools saved my life," he told them. They went back to work with a new sense of meaning and compassion.

Learning leaders realize it makes an impact in their own lives too. As leaders courageously embark on their own learning journeys, they gain confidence. They see growth in their abilities to lead. You don't go to work to check boxes; you show up to make a difference, to have an impact. You discover a new definition of success, unlocking potential all around you.

Make Work Meaningful with Shared Purpose

John Katzenbach and Douglas Smith, in their influential book, *The Wisdom of Teams*, identify a shared purpose and deliverable goal as the first characteristic necessary for forming a true team.[5] The common purpose motivates individuals to work together.

A shared purpose focuses on specific customers' needs and aspirations. The purpose builds alignment. When everyone commits to their shared purpose, the team becomes more confident and potent. Sustaining the whole team gains importance. There's less need for self-protection. People focus on customer satisfaction over blame, control, or even egos (Figure 3.1).

High-performance teams need to understand how they fit within the overall strategy. Discuss customer or stakeholder needs, benefits, and aspirations, then develop a purpose that is large enough to encompass the entire team.

Recall the purpose from the story at the beginning of this chapter.

Figure 3.1 Leadership through Learning

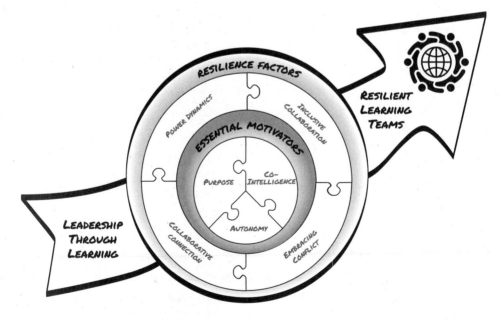

> *"Our company's customers choose our products because we innovate. We innovate because we ensure our employees have the best work environment."*

Having this shared purpose helped the team align. They found their place in the bigger organizational strategy. They chose to assume responsibility for delivering an excellent experience for candidates and employees. This included recruiting, onboarding, and sustaining the employee-company contract. While keeping the purpose front and center, they sought and found innovative ways to ensure compliance with regulations.

As teams evolve, the significance of purpose evolves too. A resilient learning team's shared goal has to be beyond functional business alignment. Their purpose may include a reason behind the goal. Their purpose may include a sense of compassion for others. Their purpose may include a desired end state. Ultimately, the purpose needs to inspire and motivate by creating a meaningful impact.

> *"Our company's customers choose our products because we innovate. We innovate because we ensure our employees have the best work environment. We lead the industry in HR practices that support learning leaders developing high levels of engagement."*

A sense of a worthwhile purpose encourages a team's journey of discovering value together. The last sentence of this purpose provides personal motivation. It links to the team's desire to take a place as thought leaders in their industry. It is specific to their goal of making a difference.

There is a collective sense of pride in courageously persisting until the team delivers. There is a collective sense of pride in making a beneficial, meaningful impact, which only further reinforces the resiliency of the team.

Moving Forward Together

A shared, meaningful purpose contributes to the team's ability to move forward together. Each successful collaboration requires engagement and shared responsibility that move the team toward the goal. Each shared achievement builds team and leader confidence. When the team has shared ownership, their actions reflect responsibility for every aspect of the work.

Team ownership includes ownership over work process, work product, and product quality. The team owns the organizational relationships with stakeholders that inform their work. This helps a resilient learning team move forward into the next successful collaboration.

It is not enough to jointly determine assignment of an action item. If the team expects individual execution of all action items, they have fostered the potential for blame. At the same time, it's true that every team member doesn't have to work on every single action item. Is the whole team overall engaging and supporting the implementation moving forward? Does anyone on the team have the ability to engage others to help move forward?

Pat, a designer, noticed diminishing morale on the team. The schedule for product release had led to everyone feeling overworked and underappreciated. Small disagreements between team members had turned to grumbling. They had worked hard for several months, and the last three weeks had been the hardest of all. Pat decided something had to be done to break the downward morale cycle. The product would bring exciting, innovative features to the marketplace. Their customers were going to love this version. But the team had lost sight of this shared, meaningful purpose.

Pat looked around for an idea and noticed something that everyone else had missed. She got online, found the website, and put in an order.

"We've got too much to do! We don't have time for this!" Team members reluctantly left their workstations. When all 12 team members had assembled, Pat whipped the tablecloth off the cart and said, "No one noticed, but we've passed an important milestone. As a team, we have not broken the build even once in the last six weeks. I've brought cupcakes (some gluten-free) and drinks for everyone!" One of the team members shouted, "Cheers!"

Pat's initiative worked. People finished their treats and went back to work feeling reenergized and refreshed. Pat heard laughter as teammates compared the tastiness of the different cupcake flavors. Work that had slowed picked up with new vigor. The team delivered on time and felt proud of their effort. Pat's leadership from within the team had done the trick.

Leadership through learning may emerge from within the team. In the foregoing story, Pat could have worried that this effort to reenergize would flop. She could have been concerned about upsetting people with the "distraction." They could have let their worries get in the way of taking action. But she felt compassion after learning about what the team was experiencing. So she looked for opportunities to celebrate small increments of progress toward delivering on the purpose. Pat role-modeled courage by observing an issue and making a choice to help the team move forward.

Learning leaders understand that alignment is not a one-time event. They embrace the complexity that meaningful, shared purposes evolve over time. And they show confidence in the team's ability to learn and move forward together to any re-aligned goals.

But What If . . . ?

- *The team or team members have many unprioritized goals?* Continuing to load new goals on teams traps us in the "full plate" dysfunction. Imagine you're at a picnic, and someone gives you a doubled-up paper plate and walks you over to the barbeque buffet. You start by serving yourself the salads—a little potato salad with dill. Add a bite or two of Grandma's macaroni salad or her feelings will be hurt. And Uncle Saul's five-bean salad (he's so proud of it). Oh, you must have some mixed-green salad too, for your healthy diet. Then you come to the cornbread, buttery garlic bread, and hot dishes. Here you add a scoop of baked beans and another of succotash. It's all so good! Right? Finally, you get to the protein. Yuki brought barbecued tofu. Fran grilled portobellos, and the hosts offered up chicken, ham-burgers, and ribs. Where is your plate now? Most likely, it bent in half sometime after the succotash. A lot of that delicious goodness slid off onto the lawn. Stop it! Every successful picnic guest knows you can't keep adding more to the plate. Instead, you have to take a few servings and finish those before going back for more. When you've identified a new goal for the team, take time to assess what prior goal, or part of it, you'll take off their "plate." How important is this new pur-pose? Will it give more or less value than what they are working on now? Adjust goal setting for competence, capacity, and the unknowns of complexity. Otherwise, you set the team up for the inevitable collapse as their plate gives way. Also, listen to the team. If they tell you their plate is close to full, pay attention. Allow for resilience and learning. When the team has no slack, team members have no flexibility when something goes wrong. Assume you can't know what will go wrong, but that something will. Flexibility produces better results.

- *Cross-team dependencies muddy responsibility of purpose and deliverables?*
  Remember the game of pickup sticks (also known as *mikado*)? While you're adjusting your expectations for goal setting, also adjust for goal clarity. As far as possible, delineate the work boundaries for as few dependencies as possible. Keep the work separate whenever you can. Create a team purpose that is independent of other teams. When this isn't possible, assume that work will take more time for cross-team coordination and communication. Develop a purpose that includes ensuring the success of the dependent team. Then be transparent about the complications of working across teams or departments.

- *The team doesn't find the shared goal motivating?*
  Get curious. Ask team members what parts of the purpose or other motivators are missing. What is present in their work environment that contributes to demotivation? Perhaps their skills aren't a good match for the work. Perhaps the goal is beyond their team capacity. Perhaps the complexity associated with the goal obscures a path to success. Do you like to embark on a task when you have no chance of succeeding? We

don't. Remember, whenever low motivation shows up, disengagement isn't far behind. Sit down with the team together and with team members individually. Seek the source of the apathy about the goal. Don't expect progress until you have removed the obstacles in the way of energized work.

- *We have employees who want to be told what to do and don't care why?*
  Sadly, people find themselves working in situations of learned helplessness. They've had unfavorable past experiences that fostered blame or shame. They learned not to bother and just demand assignments. They stopped caring about why anything was being created. Or they have more compelling purposes and interests outside work. When leaders assume demotivated employees are the problem, change is nearly insurmountable. The question becomes, Is this a situation in which you want a leadership role? What will be your purpose? Be compassionate and encourage a sense of team investment in moving forward. Everyone is motivated by something. Get curious about what would help and support them.

Reflections for Your Learning

Begin aligning on the benefits today. Learning leaders focus intensely on resilient learning for the organization, teams, and themselves.

How do you perceive the value of the external benefits of focusing on learning?
Which internal benefits would give the greatest impact?
How could you and your peers benefit?

How have you or your teams experienced a shared, meaningful purpose?

How have your teams continued aligning to move forward?

How do the Learning Leaders 4Cs (compassion, complexity, confidence, and courage) affect alignment?

CHAPTER 4

The Strategy of Continuous Learning

E ven with purpose and autonomy established, the challenges with enabling business agility are daunting. The last essential motivator is increasing co-intelligence via the strategy of continuous learning.

Continuous Learning

Leaders who nurture and encourage continuous learning demonstrate the importance of ongoing improvement. They apply this for themselves, for employees, and for every part of the organization.

Continuous learning creates a new competitive advantage when the learning transfers among others. Continuous learning not only means seeking the best sources for acquiring knowledge and skills. It also means searching for better ways to transfer that information. We want to spread what we've learned quickly and accurately from one person or team to another. Learning leaders encourage continuous learning to achieve continuous improvement efforts.

"Continuous improvement ... is the ongoing improvement of products, services or processes. ... These efforts can seek 'incremental' improvement

over time or 'breakthrough' improvement all at once,"
according to the American Society for Quality.[1]

Improvement extends across products and services, customer value, processes, and more. In knowledge work, learning has a central role in improvement. It's no longer a separate activity. A focus on continuous learning generates awareness of new possibilities, options, and alternatives. As leader Melissa Daimler wrote in *Harvard Business Review* in March 2016, "Organizational learning has to become less about the kind of learning done in a training session and more about . . . creating a work environment that supports and encourages learning. One that's less about individuals learning new skills on their own and more about using their environment to learn and learning from one another."[2]

This need for expanding continuous learning leads to **co-intelligence** as an essential motivator.

Competence and Co-Intelligence

Each team member carries their own competence and experiences that benefit their teams. Some individual team members achieve mastery by reaching the highest level of a competence. Resilient learning teams proactively build their co-intelligence. Co-intelligence is the integrated sum of skills, knowledge, and experiences of all team members. Resilient learning team members proactively share, transfer, and receive knowledge, skills, and abilities. Learning leaders amplify continuous learning during these interactions to build co-intelligence. It works both ways. Increasing a team's co-intelligence expands individual competence and solidifies mastery.

Competence describes implicit, internalized, individual knowledge, skills, and qualifications needed to accomplish a purpose. Competence that matches well to the need for skills is "fluency."

Mastery implies competence at the highest level of expertise, along with the ability to teach or mentor others. It is also known as proficiency, advanced competence, or expertise in a skill or subject area. The quest for mastery is one of the three essential motivators for individuals.

Co-intelligence is the integrated sum of skills, knowledge, and experience of all team members, as well as what can emerge from the combination, that is freely shared among the whole team. It is the total of competence and mastery the team possesses and can draw on from its members. It increases each team member's understanding of how together they contribute to team success. It unlocks new wisdom and abilities by combining the competencies. The synergy adds to greater team creativity and innovative thinking. The quest for co-intelligence is one of the three essential motivators for teams.

Relying on one's own competence and mastery is no longer enough in today's fast-changing world. In knowledge work, people must also rely on a network of expertise beyond their own sphere of ability.

Diana had never considered herself a marketing whiz. But her decades of experience in marketing her skills had served her well. She even had a marketing theory. She called it "metaphysical marketing." Her theory included showing up at events and meeting new people. She valued the hallway conversations at conferences and personal discussions at speaking engagements. Diana's theory depended on her ability to create and sustain working relationships.

When COVID-19 restrictions hit, Diana had a leadership role as cofounder of a business. This role involved managing an office staff, delivering courses, and coordinating a community of licensed coaches. Suddenly, her previously competent skills with marketing and remote interactions were no longer adequate.

Diana set out to discover what she already knew that would apply in the all-virtual setting. She explored her knowledge gaps and where she could learn the new competencies she was missing. She began reaching out to those whose expertise in these areas exceeded her own. Diana asked colleagues to recommend learning resources. She enlisted staff members with similar interests to develop a community of learners. She found opportunities to practice new skills in safe-to-fail settings. She learned her way through the shift in priorities for the business. And she's still learning.

The payoff for Diana came in the form of a deeper understanding. Her business now had a broader reach while maintaining a sense of integrity and authenticity. And she received something she valued even more: stronger networks. She reached out to tap into the knowledge and skills of others in her community. They also learned from her by exchanging skills and experiences. She developed a team of people in her company. Together, they formed their co-intelligence.

Learning leaders prioritize continuous team learning by emphasizing co-intelligence over individual competence and mastery. Teams of people that seek co-intelligence gain greater capacity. They win and their networks win. It seems like a no-brainer to work this way. Yet even so, we hesitate to devote the time and attention necessary to build co-intelligence.

Learning Inhibitors and Reactions to "Failure"

Everyone has their own idiosyncratic set of issues with learning. Yours might include one or more of the following.

Learning takes time. And time seems like a commodity in short supply. Yet when we realize that learning is the work, we can't afford to not take the time. We understand that taking time to sharpen the saw pays off in less time wasted.

Learning is an unpleasant experience. Past associations with negative "learning" experiences get in the way. Interactions have created experiences for people that link learning with blame or shame, sometimes by their teachers, by peers, or by institutional policies. Until they attain new learning experiences, this link remains.

Learning is selfish. "I can't take time for my own learning. I must devote myself to tasks or the needs of others. It would be selfish." Or, "Our manager won't give permission for us to take time for learning. She wants us to stay on task and focus on what's best for the company." No matter how these statements took root, they

A quote attributed to Abraham Lincoln: "Give me six hours to cut down a tree and I will spend the first four hours sharpening my saw." It's an analogy appreciated by woodcutters and lumberjacks everywhere. It speaks to the need to take time to prepare, especially before attempting a rigorous task in a rapidly changing landscape. Trying to work with outdated information or skills is like chopping with a blunted blade. Staying current is necessary.

are limiting people. Knowledge work is learning work. We cannot provide what is best for the business without preparing ourselves. This means dedicating ourselves to continuous learning.

Learning makes us look foolish. No one learns a new skill without going through the awkward, "I don't know how to do this yet," stage. Everyone needs time to practice achieving competence. Practice never looks perfect. So we can reframe our ideas about looking "foolish." Understand that the learning cycle means "trying something new, failing, awkwardly trying again." Get playful with learning and enjoy the foolishness.

Learning means change. When we learn something new, we can never go back to being the person we were before the learning. It will affect the way we see the world. And with each change, we perceive new things we need to learn. It's an endless cycle. Choosing learning also means choosing a willingness to change. Carol Dweck, Stanford professor and author of *Mindset: The New Psychology of Success*, has written extensively about growth versus fixed mindsets.[3] A person with a fixed mindset exhibits a tendency to assume predetermined talent. Thus, trying to learn beyond one's talent is a useless effort. A person with a growth mindset knows that change and improvement are possible, that resilience and results are achieved through the effort of learning.

Learning means we might have to share the credit for work. Traditional education and business often rely on individual competence. For people accustomed to those environments, team learning muddies the credit. A focus on stronger co-intelligence means no one individual is standing out, and thus that the team succeeds or fails. This is especially problematic during review cycles. When reviews take only individual effort into consideration, it becomes a mixed message.

Learning means admitting we don't know it all. This one may be the hardest for leaders and experts. When we've achieved the status of a leader, others look to us for answers. We discover that not knowing has power as well. According to Adam Grant, author of *Think Again: The Power of Knowing What You Don't Know*, "What we want to attain is confident humility: having faith in our capability while appreciating that we may not have the right solution or even be addressing the right problem. That gives us enough doubt to reexamine our old knowledge and enough confidence to pursue new insights."[4] Or as Rosabeth Moss Kanter, a management guru and Harvard Business School professor, asserts, "Leaders are more powerful when they learn than when they teach."[5]

Learning means we have to admit failure. The path to learning lies through aspiration and pain. This happens when we don't know how to do this new thing yet, or when we try something, and bad things happen. To get the most benefits from learning, we must reframe failure. We shift away from blaming and shaming because we didn't achieve a successful outcome. Instead, we regard it as an opportunity to learn. We examine how to mitigate and improve in future situations. Failure becomes a signal of the need for more or new learning. It still may feel like an undesirable loss. We may fear another one. Yet the way to deal with fear and gain resilience is to learn our way through it.

A paradox accompanies all these inhibitors. You may have experiences that back these failures up as true. Yet the way to break free from these is through learning. To keep up with the changing world, build co-intelligence. When people mention lifelong learning, this is what they mean. It's unavoidable. So let's get good at it!

Build Co-intelligence with Five Rules of Learning

With a foundation of individual continuous learning, teams begin building co-intelligence through collaboration. Collaboration occurs when two or more people work together to achieve a goal. Collaborative work leverages the wisdom of the team to discover new ways to meet a common goal. Through collaboration,

When Tricia works with a team, she introduces the "how fascinating moment" technique. She borrowed the technique from Rosamund Stone Zander and Benjamin Zander's book, *The Art of Possibility: Transforming Professional and Personal Life*.[6] It's likely also familiar to people who've studied improv acting techniques as an adapted form of "the failure bow."

When anyone makes a mistake, whether silly or serious, we pause to notice it. Instead of assuming a guilty stance or hunching our shoulders in shame, we stand up straight. We acknowledge that something unexpected has occurred. We recognize it as an opportunity. How fascinating it is to discover this opportunity to learn something new! We throw our hands into the air, lift our heads, and shout, "How fascinating!" three times. Others can join in. Then, we immediately get to work learning. We learn whatever we need to improve the situation. It counters the tendency to blame with acknowledgment while taking responsibility.

the team finds actions that no individual could produce alone. Collaboration is "our part," not "your part, my part." It takes time to develop a rhythm in collaborations and continuous learning.

Alistair Cockburn, Agile Manifesto author and founder of Heart of Agile, states, "In the workshops I run on improving collaboration, people's ideas largely fall into two buckets: attitude, and mechanics. Attitude is whether anyone even wants to collaborate, and how much energy they are willing to put into it. Fear is a top entry in this category. Mechanics are all the factors that make it easy or hard, effective or not. Distance, technologies and overcommitted schedules are entries in this category. This is a great exercise to run in any reflection workshop."[7] As authors, we experienced these two buckets ourselves.

The amount of time it took to write the first draft of one of the chapters of this book was almost painful. We have known and respected each other for many years. But working closely together was different. We had to learn about each other's goals for writing. We had to explore where we agreed on our purpose and where we differed. We learned what we were both passionate about and what we each preferred in our interactions. The pain was more in the length of time it took to complete a task than in the interactions. But we understood that there is no short-cut to building collaboration. It takes time, effort, and interest. We had the right attitude for establishing respect and trust. We maximized team learning and shared responsibility, thus minimizing the inclination for blame.

As we saw the book take shape, we knew that neither of us could have done it alone. Over time, as we collaborated, we built our co-intelligence. We learned information the other person had. We created new ideas. We discovered the mechanics that work well for us. Then one day, we realized we could accomplish so much in a short block of time (Figure 4.1).

Figure 4.1 Leadership through Learning

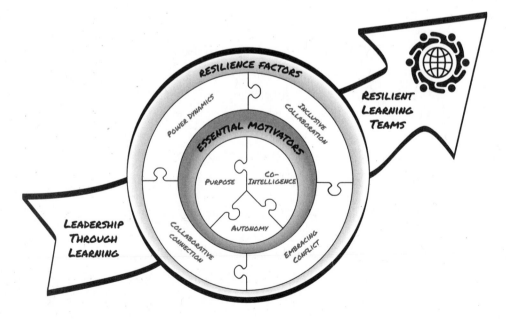

Learning leaders make it safe to admit the need to learn individually and together. Experts have published countless guidelines and recommendations for teaching and learning as individuals. There is less written about building co-intelligence in teams. To create the right conditions for building co-intelligence, they use the five rules of learning.

In their book, *Five Rules of Accelerated Learning*, Willem Larsen and Diana Larsen incorporate many streams of thought about learning and how to encourage others' learning.[8] They identified the five fundamental rules (Figure 4.2 and Table 4.1):

Figure 4.2 Five Rules for Accelerated Learning

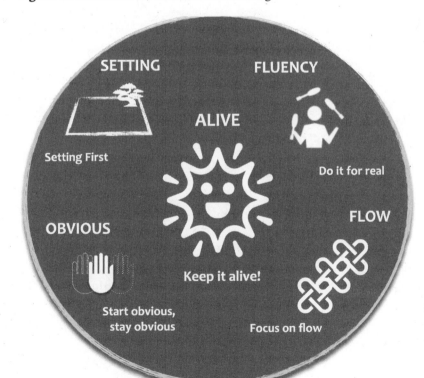

Table 4.1 Five Rules for Accelerated Learning

ALIVE—Keep it alive!

Main Purpose: To generate energy for learning

Introduction
The rule of Alive contains within it the entire universe of coherent, deep learning. Lasting learning comes from full engagement and a sense of urgency. This means generating energy for learning is the grandmother rule to all other rules.

Notes
Full engagement looks like joy, play, eyes wide open, and body fully present. It's shown in rapt attention and learners who are in the intensity of the moment. It appeals to human senses. It emerges from relationships. Remember moments when you have felt alive and engaged. Immerse yourself in the memory. Re-create the vividness, emotion, intensity, and physicality. Notice your sense of discovery. Notice what sensory or relationship connections occurred. Notice your connection to nature or beauty.

Urgency arises from needs, as well as desires. Needs demand response. Learners may express need through curiosity, motivation, or a sense of purpose or responsibility. Learning needs come from aspirations, deadlines, surprises, or crises. Full engagement promotes taking responsibility over obligation.

The Questions
When have I seen instances of keeping it alive in my workplace? What strength do I bring to keeping it alive for those I lead? What's one more thing I could do to foster aliveness? What's another?

SETTING—Attend to the setting first

Main Purpose: To first foster a learning environment

Introduction
To create maximum learning, widen the focus beyond relationships. In addition to leader and team relationships, look at the environment. Kurt Lewin's formula asserts that human behavior is a function of the person in their environment.[a] They are not separate. To optimize learning, we must attend to the setting first. This includes in-person, physical settings and remote, virtual settings.

Table 4.1 *(continued)*

SETTING—Attend to the setting first

Notes
The setting may include physical space, virtual space and platforms, artifacts, and access to equipment or tools. It provides an environment for appealing to human senses with color, use of body, or tactile experience—even taste. Attend to the setting in accord with all the other rules. Think about setting early on as a way to mitigate Murphy's law ("Whatever can go wrong will go wrong").[b] Become a sleuth. Look for clues in the setting that could disrupt learning.

The Questions
When have you seen a great setting for learning at work? What conditions were present? What about this setting hinders or enables coherent learning? Is the temperature just right? Is there background noise? Is the workspace arranged in a way that helps or hampers conversation? Do you have the right tools for learning? What about the setting promotes psychological safety?

FLUENCY—Do it for real

Main Purpose: To gain internalized experience

Introduction
To collaborate well, teams need skills in learning, thinking, and making decisions together. We do it for real to gain internalized experience in the knowledge and skills we need. Fluency is empirical and observable, signaling the presence of competency and co-intelligence. You know it when you see it. You know it when you feel it. You feel it when you have achieved it. Fluency shows itself even under pressure.

Notes
Talk is cheap, but true competent action compels respect. Action demonstrates practiced experience and ability. No doubt you want that for yourself. No doubt you want it for those you lead. When learners perform skills as they learn them, even haltingly or awkwardly, this is doing it for real. Fluency proficiency shows up as routine, skillful ease. Unfortunately, many institutions tend to focus on gaining knowledge rather than fluency. Too often they teach "about" skills. Instructors "expose" students to information and facts, without encouraging the skills of application.

As learners gain fluency together, co-intelligence builds. This experience promotes shared responsibility.

(continued)

Table 4.1 *(continued)*

FLUENCY—Do it for real

The Questions
What fluency do you want the team to build? When do you support "do it for real"? Where is it missing? What further ways to grow and maintain fluency do you want to learn for yourself? What fluency do you want to gain by doing it for real?

OBVIOUS—Start obvious and stay obvious

Main Purpose: To maintain momentum for learning

Introduction
Obvious, like the signal strength and reception of a broadcast station, indicates the ratio of clarity to noise. Any trickery, intentional ambiguity, distraction, or guessing gets in the way of learning. We don't want noise. We want clear intentions and momentum for learning.

Notes
We remove all noise from a learning design and from the setting. We throw trickery and "testing people" right out the window. Diagnose the appropriate level of obviousness by asking a simple question: Do you observe even an iota of hesitancy in the teams' behavior? If so, get clearer.

Find the right balance. Too much obviousness leads to boredom. Too little, and lack of clarity leads to panic and a feeling of being overwhelmed. The right degree of obviousness leads to an ease for continuous learning. This ease promotes shared responsibility.

The Questions
Where does obvious apply for learning in your workplace? When do you perceive obvious handled well? Where and when do team members hesitate to engage? What impedes obviousness or masks clarity?

FLOW—Focus on flow

Main Purpose: To increase skill for greater co-intelligence

Introduction
Competence comes from practice. So while we must "do it for real" to internalize the experience, we also need to start with basics and build on the skills in a coherent flow or sequence. Focus on flow by reducing chunks of skill to their core, then sequence them in order of need. Start with the smallest valuable chunk of skill that makes sense. Eventually, add nuance

Table 4.1 *(continued)*

FLOW—Focus on flow

and more technique to the learning infrastructure to build skills. Each new skill team members acquire adds to the whole team's co-intelligence.

Notes
Let's imagine you find yourself in a fully alive environment and setting for learning. You observe real fluent action. There seems to be enough obviousness, with no ambiguity or hesitation from the team. Yet still you are not seeing an increase in skill. There is only one thing left to do—focus on flow.

Consider the complexity and size of the chunks of learning and the sequence. First, ensure fluent ease with the current skill. After achieving this skill, intentionally add the next obvious "bite-size pieces" to absorb. Avoid unnecessary or extended challenges. Think of it as building upward, to higher and more complex levels of proficiency. If you build the widest base possible, learners will never move up. But with a too-narrow base, learners will never have enough to build on.

In the end, flow will speed up their (and your) learning and building of co-intelligence.

The Questions
Where have you seen effective examples of flow elsewhere in your work? How could you use a better flow to boost continuous learning and improvement? Are your team members choking on oversize pieces of learning? Are the pieces coming too fast or in an order that doesn't make sense?

Source: Adapted from *Five Rules of Accelerated Learning*, by Willem Larsen and Diana Larsen. ©2016, 2021.
[a] https://en.wikipedia.org/wiki/Lewin%27s_equation.
[b] https://en.wikipedia.org/wiki/Murphy%27s_law.

- Alive—to generate energy for learning
- Setting—to first foster a learning environment
- Fluency—to gain internalized experience
- Obvious—to maintain momentum for learning
- Flow—to increase skill for greater co-intelligence

In complex and chaotic environments, these rules will help with diagnosing learning issues. Apply them to set continuous learning conditions at work, in meetings, in coaching, or in mentoring. Apply them when the team has identified an area in which to build expertise. As the team collaborates and learns together, their co-intelligence expands. And as the learning leader, you will gain and demonstrate confidence in your team's learning abilities.

Leadership through learning embraces continuous team learning. Learning leaders show the courage to invoke a growth mindset and feel awkward, clumsy, or halting during learning. They demonstrate that they are compassionate about learning inhibitors by intentionally creating the right conditions for success.

But What If . . . ?

- *Senior management doesn't support me in expecting teams to have time to learn?*
  As a leader, your success likely depends on whether your teams meet expectations. When you know that learning is a key component for work, you want your teams to learn as needed. In conversations, reframe "teams taking time to learn" as "teams doing their work." Avoid characterizing learning as an activity separate from production work. It's not.
- *HR demands a focus on individual performance, in reviews and through policies?*
  A focus on individual performance holds a destructive sway over effective teamwork. Where possible, spend whatever social capital you've accumulated to shift the policy. If you've been unsuccessful, acknowledge it with your teams. Look for ways to mitigate the impact. Ask teams how they'd like recognition collectively for their work. Add your own questions in performance reviews.

Drew Bryan, chief information officer, offered, "A team can come together and collaborate on each person's contributions as a team member as well as recommendations on personal growth. A manager can capture these in the review still using a team-based model, but adhering to the rigid HR structure."[9] But don't give up on that organizational change. Begin documenting instances when the work was only accomplished through collaboration. Change the narrative.

- *Teams won't produce if they don't fear punishment for failures?*
When team members experience blame, they find it difficult to imagine alternatives. Fear is only a temporary motivator and loses its production impact over time. Unfortunately, the emotional impact is lasting, often leading to the next level of reactions, including apathy and despair. When we encounter these situations, we look for ways to energize the teams. With enough new positive experiences, beliefs and assumptions begin to alter.

- *People want to remain experts in their existing areas only (territorial or fear)?*
This phenomenon seems to arise from one of two sources. The person may ascribe to the fixed mindset. It leads them to believe they have no other option beyond their current expertise, that there is no value in collaboration. Or they have interests outside the current workstream. They may want to focus any new learning on those outside interests. On resilient learning teams, this won't be an acceptable state. To discover which source affects them, have an honest conversation. Once you know, you can discuss their options. One option may be to find them a different position that is better suited for individuals or groups.

- *I get pressure to measure whether my teams get it perfect the first time?*

  Since perfection is unattainable, your teams will never achieve it. We can't expect perfection. We can expect a good enough result for the team to keep learning what is next to align and move forward. Take the focus off "perfect." Instead, focus on satisfying customer needs. It may also be an unattainable goal, but it's more gratifying when the team gets closer and closer over time.

Reflections for Your Learning

Begin your strategy of continuous learning to build co-intelligence today. Learning leaders focus intensely on resilient learning for the organization, teams, and themselves.

How does continuous learning appear in your organization?

How does continuous learning appear in your behavior?

How has co-intelligence influenced your career path?

How are learning inhibitors and reactions getting in the way?

How might you seek greater co-intelligence with the five rules?

How do the Learning Leaders 4Cs (compassion, complexity, confidence, and courage) impact co-intelligence?

CHAPTER 5

Accelerating the Essential Motivators with Retrospectives

With attention to the three essential motivators, leaders point the way toward becoming a resilient learning team. In *Project Retrospectives: A Handbook for Team Review*, Norman L. Kerth presents a shift to focusing on a systemic view rather than seeking individual fault. The "retrospective prime directive" best illustrates this shift in thinking:

> *"Regardless of what we discover, we understand and truly believe that everyone did the best job they could, given what they knew at the time, their skills and abilities, the resources available, and the situation at hand."*[1]

The fallacy that all issues are preventable wastes valuable time. Yet people continue down this unhealthy path because of hindsight bias. Hindsight bias, known as the we-knew-it-all-along phenomenon, arises from the common tendency for people to perceive past events as having been more predictable than they actually were.[2] In knowledge work, rarely can we point to a single, simple source at fault. The reality is there are unknown unknowns.

Leadership through learning is centered on building resilient learning teams. Every interaction offers an opportunity to be a learning leader. To lay a foundation for enabling high performance, learning leaders focus on amplifying the essential motivators of purpose, co-intelligence, and autonomy. Particularly, we regard retrospectives as a wonderful opportunity to accelerate the essential motivators' impact on the team. A retrospective event holds space for teams to build co-intelligence. Retrospectives create a setting to examine past experience and positively influence the future.

To start, retrospective leaders guide a team as they learn about their collective experiences. Team members share their perspectives. They create one common story built on all the data available. Then the leader assists the team in analyzing the implications together. That brings the team to collaboratively choose the next improvement actions. This valuable framework emphasizes learning about the system and how to influence it for better outcomes.

On a cool autumn evening in London, Diana attended a preconference networking event. Wine and canapés flowed as the group of speakers and conference organizers mingled. She felt a tap on her shoulder. She turned to see a young man who looked familiar. Daniel reintroduced himself. He had participated in a retrospective leaders' workshop she led several months earlier. He confided, "Since then, I've learned the secret of retrospectives." Surprised that anyone thought she had held back, she responded, "And which secret is that?"

Daniel explained that as the team became better at participating in retrospectives, their skills improved in other meetings too. They had learned about the retrospective prime directive, and they now embraced it throughout the entire day. They gained confidence in their ability to learn their way through any situa-

tion. And the more they collaborated and learned together, the less finger-pointing was a part of their team.

Needless to say, Diana shared her delight about Daniel's application of what he'd learned.

Well-run retrospectives support improvements in all the "despicable" parts of meetings and interactions. These improvements help shift the team to responsibility with autonomy, align toward a shared purpose, benefit from continuous learning to build co-intelligence, and more. The more you spread retrospectives across the teams, the more you build responsibility and resiliency.

Retrospectives for Resilience Framework

Improvement events are an existing leadership technique—for example, Lessons Learned, Post Mortems, After Action Reviews, and many others. But too often, these events become judgmental competitions to avoid attention and responsibility. Or worse, they become hero-worship sessions. These approaches are more beneficial than no reflection at all. Yet we prefer retrospectives because, when led well, they don't foster blame.

The book *Agile Retrospectives: Making Good Teams Great*, by Esther Derby and Diana Larsen, popularized an improvement framework for software development teams.[3] Unfortunately, retrospectives became viewed as only an information technology team technique, which is not what the authors intended. Thus, retrospectives remain underutilized within organizations as a whole.

A retrospective can help a team step back, reassess, and plan a way forward. In organizations that value and focus on continuous improvement, favorable opportunities become clear. And no two retrospectives are the same. Retrospectives can support many different situations at work (Figure 5.1).

Figure 5.1 Retrospective Types

	Cadence: 30 mins to 1 month Frequent regular	Cadence: quarterly to annually Intermittent	Cadence: yearly to only once Rarely
Individual/pair	**Event:** Completed a work increment. **Intent:** Want to assess collaboration before starting the next increment.		
Single group/team		**Event:** Completed a special project. **Intent:** Improve how to approach future projects.	**Event:** Controversy, challenge, conflict, or impediment slows the team's work. **Intent:** Build whole group learning and alignment.
N groups/teams		**Event:** Produced a major deliverable. **Intent:** Reflect with everyone engaged in the release.	**Event:** Reorganization creates dramatic shifts that alters team makeups. **Intent:** New teams' members want to reset and clarify expectations.
X-organization		**Event:** Unexpected event creates a major disruption, stops team's work, and interrupts the product plan. **Intent:** Reflect and examine alternatives to help team regain momentum.	**Event:** Leadership decides to sunset a product (end-of-sales or end-of-life). **Intent:** Everyone wants to improve their processes for new products.

For example, a team may hold short, very frequent retrospectives. Through these they gain quick, small improvement ideas. Alternatively, a team may need a longer retrospective to find past work patterns in order to consider a significant change.

Retrospectives are effective for the following:

- executive teams
- management teams
- departments
- teams
- workflows
- during or at the end of a project or initiative
- unexpected events
- stakeholder engagement

There are an infinite number of retrospective topics. The following are some examples:

- How could we improve our communication with marketing?
- Do we have the best makeup of skills on the team?
- How are our simple rules or working agreements serving us?
- How can we best support each other in our professional development?
- What have we learned from this project that could build success in the future?
- How will we incorporate the best aspects of the cross-department work into our next effort?
- This updated team composition means we have a new team. What do we want to carry forward, and what do we want to try that is new?
- How can we regain our momentum by resolving our differences?
- What are opportunities in working from home due to the pandemic?

Figure 5.2 Retrospectives for Resilience

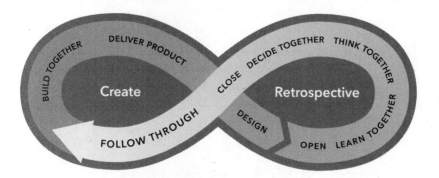

For learning leaders, we've expanded the retrospective steps from Derby and Larsen's *Agile Retrospectives* (Figure 5.2).

The Retrospective for Resilience Framework provides a container for continuous learning. The framework opens by reinforcing the benefits of a shared purpose. Autonomy increases with the easy flow for teams to think, learn, and decide on specific actions together. Participants show generous appreciation for each other's contributions and collaborative idea generation, thus building co-intelligence.

Yet if people go through the motions, they won't experience these benefits. To do this well, leaders must learn to be facilitators building responsibility within teams. Leaders won't always be the right person to guide the retrospective process. But an understanding of facilitation will assist you in choosing the right facilitator.

The Leader as a Facilitator

Facilitation is the art and craft of engaging others' wisdom toward achieving an outcome. Facilitation skills incorporate designing the flow *before* the event, shepherding the team *during* it, and following up on the next steps *after* it.

[Facilitation] is the body of expertise associated with cooperation and collaboration among equals, and is concerned with ways of ensuring that everyone in a group can, if they wish, fully participate in all decisions that affect them. — The Art of Facilitation, by Dale Hunter[4]

Organizational Development uses group processes to harness the wisdom and commitment of the stakeholders to improve their own organizations. It is based on the belief that people are wise and will have more commitment to the plans or changes that they've designed for themselves. — Advanced Facilitation Strategies, by Ingrid Bens[5]

Resilient learning teams take shared responsibility for the next steps. But to align, collaborate, and decide, a team often benefits from neutral help to move forward. Hence the need for a facilitator.

A facilitator creates a setting with consideration for psychological safety. They design the flow of interactions. A facilitator makes the collaboration easier. Not easy, necessarily, but easier than it would be otherwise. They shepherd a space for everyone to collaborate toward a shared outcome. To achieve success as a facilitator, they stay neutral on the outcome.

A facilitator is a person who helps a group of people to work together better, understand their common objectives, and plan how to achieve these objectives, during meetings or discussions. In doing so, the facilitator remains "neutral," meaning he/she does not take a particular position in the discussion. — Wikipedia[6]

[A facilitator is] a person who is acceptable to all group members, substantively neutral, and has no decision-making authority who helps a group improve the way it identifies and solves problems and makes decisions. — The Skilled Facilitator[7]

The facilitator's job is to support everyone to do their best thinking and practice. By supporting everyone to do their best thinking, a facilitator enables group members to search for inclusive solutions and build sustainable agreements. — Sam Kaner[8]

Neutrality is critical for teams to take responsibility for their co-intelligence and autonomy. When a leader is not a neutral facilitator, they will send mixed messages to the team. When a leader takes a neutral stance, acting as the facilitator demonstrates confidence in the team's abilities. As Roger Schwarz *states* "You do not have to give up your leadership role or your expertise to use facilitative skills. On the contrary; using facilitative skills enhances your leadership."[9]

Example

Facilitators are more than the people at the front of the room. Let's examine how one facilitator uses the Retrospective for Resilience Framework.

> For the last year, a nine-person executive team has met monthly to examine their performance. Initially, they made several quick improvements. Lately, they have fallen back into past siloed behaviors and control habits. As a result, they agreed to look for help. Each team member, including the CEO, acknowledged they couldn't stay neutral as the facilitator. So the CEO hired an external consultant, Leigh, to facilitate their next retrospective.

In this scenario, the decision to have an external facilitator is critical. If the facilitator is a decision maker or part of the team, the team's ability to collaborate diminishes. It sets up a conflict of interest and diminishes shared responsibility.

Coming from outside this executive team, Leigh assessed the situation. First, Leigh wanted to define the topic and outcome of the retrospective. Leigh met with each executive team member, and learned about individual and team aspirations and pain points. Leigh had a list of questions to ask in interviews before the retrospective.

If you're familiar with the team you are working with, consider your own answers to these questions. If you're facilitating a new team, interview people as needed. Talk to people who may offer disparate perspectives. To be clear, assessment is not about taking sides or figuring it all out up front. Assessment questions help inform logistics decisions, design decisions, and facilitation decisions.

Leigh gained insight by collecting answers to the assessment questions in Table 5.1, which are flexible depending on the situation.

Table 5.1 Example Assessment Questions

	Example assessment question	Scenario insights
Topic	What is the focus for the retrospective?	The goal is to get back on track and align toward a shared business direction and purpose collaboratively.
Neutrality	Will too much knowledge or a lack of knowledge create a challenge for the facilitator?	No. With Leigh's degree of facilitation knowledge and skills, the topic is achievable.
Background	What organizational history (issues, people, etc.) might affect this retrospective?	The founder story of the organization influences rewards for "heroic" efforts. This seems to no longer be serving everyone.
Experience	What healthy team dynamics and behaviors are occurring?	• Three of the team members have read and discussed *Turn the Ship Around!*, by L. David Marquet, and *Team of Teams*, by Stanley McChrystal.[a] These discussions have led to a shared desire to work effectively together as a team. • Leigh discovered a high mutual respect for each other's knowledge and competence. They would like to build their co-intelligence. • This team engages in one activity outside work each month. • Everyone agrees that recent retrospectives have not been productive. • Team members want to help each other.

Table 5.1 *(continued)*

	Example assessment question	Scenario insights
	What unhealthy team dynamics and behaviors are occurring?	• While the intent is to help, many actions Leigh heard about create negative impacts for others. • Despite their mutual respect, Leigh noticed quite a few unhealthy competitive statements. There is a reluctance to share information from a few members. • Leigh identified a pattern that, until critical escalation, organizational issues remain unaddressed.
Participants	Who should or will attend?	Everyone was invited. All nine people expressed a sincere willingness and commitment to attend.
	What roles will be present?	The list includes the CEO, chief operating officer, vice president of sales, vice president of marketing, director of production, vice president of information management, vice president of human resources, director of customer support, and vice president of product development.
	Which people or roles may cause challenges?	The directors' reporting relationships with vice presidents may pose issues. In addition, the following dynamics may create challenges:

(continued)

Table 5.1 *(continued)*

	Example assessment question	Scenario insights
		• The vice president of HR tends to focus on reducing legal liability over experimentation. • The vice president of sales tends to prioritize revenue results over customer and employee satisfaction. • The chief operating officer has exceeded capacity with responsibility for finance, security, legal, and operations. • As one of the founders, the CEO is a visionary. But he has an unrealistic expectation of the work necessary. This includes his own role.
Readiness	Are people prepared for this collaboration?	They are as prepared as they can be at this point.

[a] L. David Marquet, *Turn the Ship Around! A True Story of Turning Followers into Leaders* (New York: Portfolio, 2013); Stanley McChrystal, *Team of Teams: New Rules of Engagement for a Complex World* (New York: Portfolio, 2015).

With this information, Leigh designed a setting and flow promoting the essential motivators. Leigh understood there are many complexity factors for the optimal setting and design. The assessment results inform these factors. Each factor adds or removes difficulty within a retrospective (Table 5.2).

Guided by the Retrospective for Resilience Framework, Leigh's design focused on a collaborative container that emphasized team responsibility for the outcome.

Table 5.2 Retrospective Complexity Factors

• co-located or virtual	• complexity of the work (unknown territory)
• on-site or off-site location	• degree of conflict (occurred or potential)
• duration	• degree of controversy (occurred or potential)
• number of participants	• power dynamics (Can all voices be respected?)
• length of the relevant work	• psychological safety (willing to have a voice)
• length of time working together	• team fluency zone (for agile teams)
• team makeup changes	• observer demands (minimize impact)
• scale of topic	• context in the organization (circle of control)
• participants' availability and diversity	• organizational culture influences (consequences)

Retrospective Logistics
- **Setting:** In person
- **Number of participants:** Invited nine
- **Duration:** Half day (8:00 a.m.–12:00 p.m.)
- **Time and day:** Tuesday morning, with optional lunch following
- **Food:** Coffee, juice, water, breakfast trail mix
- **Location:** Off-site at nearby hotel conference room
- **Setup:** One U-shaped table set up with room around the table for small-group activities; accessory table for supplies, including flip charts, markers, sticky notes, and so on.

First, Leigh designed the logistics with an ideal setting to aid in team success, borrowing from the five rules of learning to keep the aliveness present. The nearby hotel conference room had plenty of space. There were large windows with a beautiful view and easy access to the estate grounds. Note that you do not always need a grand setting. The focus is on having natural cues in the environment that aid in a sense of calming presence and lend energy toward fostering creativity. For in-person meetings, you could borrow a potted plant. For virtual meetings, add flowers or art that suggests nature (real or a virtual effect).

Leigh chose to have all participants in person. This ensures that everyone has the same participation opportunities. The alternative would have been to have everyone be remote. When possible, we still recommend all in person over all remote. This is for a few reasons. First, humans communicate, interact, and connect with more than words alone. Communication flows easier, faster, and more accurately in person. Second, we reduce time spent (wasted) dealing with technology issues. Third, when everyone is present together, we hear and can better attend to the various voices in the room.

Retrospective Design

The retrospective design provides a process outline for the facilitator to accomplish the goal. Below, we share Leigh's design.

Set the Stage (20 Minutes)

- **Facilitator intent:** To model the ideal *setting* and energy (*alive*) for learning over blaming. To align on the topic and outcome of the retrospective, while reinforcing the team's shared *purpose*. To encourage low-risk participation, creativity, and shared desires.
- **Overall retrospective agenda**
- **Topic:** Improve executive team performance
- **Outcome:** Define one or two actions that will help the team move forward by regaining alignment on a shared business direction.

- **Activity:** Pick a picture that represents something you appreciate about this team over the past quarter. Share your picture and briefly express why you chose this image.

Gather Data (45 Minutes)

- **Facilitator intent:** To *obviously* build momentum through shared understanding of the whole team experience. To clarify that each person is important to figuring out the puzzle. To increase transfer of knowledge and begin building *co-intelligence*.
- **Activity:** Using a timeline with an x axis of the various events and goals, the team puts notes on the y axis of the timeline indicating whether the event or goal added energy or removed energy from the team. Everyone stands back a distance from the timeline to notice what they can observe—for example, an observation that the energy has been steadily declining. Then everyone examines each section of the timeline up close to notice what they can discuss. For example, the up-close observation shows that after a new goal is added, energy goes both up for some team members and down for other team members.

Break (10 Minutes)

- **Facilitator intent:** Attending to team members' physical and mental needs helps them stay energized and refreshed (*alive*) for the work.
- Encourage healthy choices such as beverages, a quick walk, and so on.

Generate Insights (75 Minutes)

- **Facilitator intent:** To encourage all voices and respectful examination and internalization of deeper issues, causes, impacts, and challenges (*fluency*). Explore feasibility of new insights and ideas emerging (*co-intelligence*).

- **Activity:** Encourage discussion of influences prompting multiple events or goals. To minimize defensiveness, use questions from the six thinking hats activity, in which, participants are assigned a hat that represents a specific way of thinking. For example, wearing a green hat means the participant will approach the discussion from a creative perspective.[10]
- **Activity:** After examining what got us here, discuss what would have to happen to get us back to alignment on a shared business direction.

Break (10 Minutes)

- **Facilitator intent:** Attending to team members' physical and mental needs helps them stay energized and refreshed (*alive*) for the work.
- Encourage healthy choices such as beverages, a quick walk, and so on.

Decide What to Do (30 Minutes)

- **Facilitator intent:** To bring the team together to achieve the outcome. To support the team *autonomy* and *responsibility* for the decision regarding their *shared purpose*.
- **Activity:** With the prompt "What will improve our team alignment by 20 percent?" each team member individually answers privately on a card. Then, in pairs, team members discuss both answers and decide collaboratively how to split seven points between the two options. They write the score on the back of each card, then swap cards with each other and find a new pair.

Repeat until all pairs have interacted. Tally up the points for each idea. Engage in a discussion on the top three to collectively decide on the final one or two actions.

Close the Retrospective (20 Minutes)

- **Facilitator intent:** To share hopes and wishes for today's retrospective (*alive*). To give feedback to the facilitator. To reinforce the team's *responsibility* for their work.
- **Reiterate commitment to action:** Owners, next step, deadline, and so on.
- **Activity:** Briefly share any hopes and wishes for the team.
- **Activity:** Indicate return on investment of time spent: high, medium, or low. Indicate any "keep" or "drop" items for the facilitator.
  Note: This retrospective event was scheduled for four hours. The design accounts for 3 hours and 30 minutes. The additional 30 minutes is buffer time for unexpected adjustments to the design. For example, the group may need more time for a discussion than was planned.

As the facilitator, Leigh embodied the Learning Leaders 4Cs in the design and during facilitation. In addition, Leigh made sure the design *flow* built on the previous pieces to enable the executive team to learn together.

In Set the Stage, Leigh set an energetic tone right from the start with a focus and thought-provoking image activity. Also, Leigh narrowed complexity by creating a focused topic and outcome. What's the right-size piece that the team can actually address? Small steps lead to small successes. Small successes build energy for the next improvement. In Gather Data, Leigh created an activity that increased awareness and compassion for different experiences over time. In Generate Insights, Leigh encouraged all voices to take the learning deeper into complexity and make it real. They courageously role-played with different perspectives. They developed an understanding of their mutual willingness, collaboration, and responsibility to find a solution. In Decide What to Do, Leigh helped the team achieve actionable steps. Leigh banned unproductive terms like less, more, lack of, and so on. The only thing you can do about "less" is get more. By getting specific, responsibility can occur. Leigh remained neutral in the decision and demonstrated confidence in the team's ability to decide. In Close the Retrospective, Leigh kept the energy high by focusing on future desires.

Despite the best designs and facilitation, retrospective participants may still fall into bad habits. The art of facilitation includes staying present in the moment. This enables the facilitator to notice and adjust, especially if blaming begins.

In the six thinking hats activity, Leigh noticed mocking between two team members, and decided to ignore this initial inappropriate behavior. As the retrospective continued, the volume of sarcastic humor and mocking increased. Soon it spread among other team members. Leigh knows that sarcastic humor, mocking, and sniping can be very dangerous to teams. This behavior may seem innocent and playful at first. Yet Leigh knows it can quickly turn to contempt and unspoken issues.

To keep the retrospective focused on continuous learning, Leigh decided to pause the discussion with a break. Breaks help to interrupt any disruptive dynamics. During the break, Leigh removed all the hats except the white hat and red hat. After the break concluded, instead of returning to the previous exercise, Leigh requested that the team take a step back to examine their interactions: "What do you notice happening in our team?" using only the white and red hats.

White hat: With this thinking hat, you focus on the available data. Look at the information that you have, analyze past trends, and see what you can learn from it. Look for gaps in your knowledge and try to either fill them or take account of them.

Red hat: With this thinking hat, you look at problems using your intuition, gut reaction, and emotion. Also think how others could react emotionally. Try to understand the responses of people who do not fully know your reasoning.[11]

Initially, the responses to this question included silence and dismissive comments. Leigh remained silent. Eventually, the vice president of sales offered, "Well, we were making progress. Yeah, there was a little ribbing or joking happening, but not a big deal. Was it?" Leigh remained silent. The chief operating officer took a deep breath and responded, "It wasn't that funny to me. My teams are absolutely worn out from being overworked. Jokes about not being able to cross the finish line are not funny." The vice president of sales quickly retorted, "Relax. We don't mean anything by it." Then the CEO leaned forward and said, "Wait. This is a good example of stuff that gets in our way of being a team. We need to be able to highlight impacts and work together to meet everyone's needs." The CEO turned to Leigh, saying, "Thank you for creating space for us to notice this." Leigh replied, "The topic of our retrospective is to regain alignment as a team. Seems like this might be an impediment to the success of the team. What are some steps that the team can take to support interaction and humor in a productive way?" The result of this discussion led the group to return to collaboration and learning.

In this example facilitation, Leigh's awareness led to an opportunity to build resiliency. Leigh chose not to intervene too early. This provided space to explore subtle, touchy issues that had remained hidden. With further observation, Leigh neutrally stepped in to help the team discuss the issue, and didn't take responsibility or sides. Instead, Leigh reinforced that the whole team shares responsibility for moving their progress forward. Leigh reinforced and accelerated the essential motivators by reminding the team of their shared purpose, by providing space for the team to increase this co-intelligence of uncovering issues and working together, and by encouraging autonomy through asking what steps they want to take.

This discussion took time that Leigh had not originally budgeted for. Yet this became a critical step they needed to achieve their retrospective topic and outcome. Leigh adjusted the rest of the design to still meet the outcome.

Well-run retrospectives reinforce that the whole team is greater than any individual. When a team learns, thinks, and decides together, shared responsibility deepens. But retrospectives don't solve problems. They provide a setting for learning leaders to help people solve their problems. Going through the motions won't guarantee results. Depending on how retrospectives are facilitated, the benefits may prove uneven. If you fall victim to hindsight bias, you won't gain the benefits. If you skip thinking, learning, or deciding, you won't gain the benefits. If you don't achieve responsibility, you won't gain the benefits.

But What If . . . ?

- *I can't get buy-in to invest this much time to do retrospectives?*
  It might seem as though every retrospective will be a
  time-consuming event. It depends on the complexity
  factors. In challenging situations, time increases for
  unpacking and reassessing the path forward. Yet
  retrospectives don't have to be time consuming to
  create effective improvements. Sometimes, the daily

small, focused micro-learnings are what can make bigger investments possible. Retrospectives need designs and facilitation that fit the scenario.

Example 1: Small teams break their work into shorter time blocks (a.k.a. *pomodoros*). They hold 1-to-5-minute "micro-retros" after each 25-minute time block. It's led by a team member, and it goes as follows:

Design: Prepare the team with the expectation that we will pause frequently to discuss what we've learned and how to improve our work.

Set the stage: Time to micro-retro before our break.

Gather data: What did we notice?

Generate insights: What's a small thing we could improve?

Decide what to do: What's a new action we could take?

Close the retrospective: Now that we've captured that, let's take a break!

Follow through: Keep track of the decided action.

Example 2: A team of four colleagues traveled to the same location for three-to-five-day work intensives. At the end of the week, they drove to the airport together. During the drive, they held a retrospective on their time together for that week. Note that the driver never facilitated (safety first!).

Example 3: Ask a single open-ended question, "What is one small thing that can help make our team, our product, or our workflow better right now?" If this conversation happens in the hallway, meetings, and so on, it reinforces reflection and learning.

Example 4: There are other ways to consider the larger investment of time required. Calculate the expense associated with holding the retrospective. What percentage of the overall budget would we be willing to spend on an activity that improves our chances of success? Then compare that amount with the cost of holding the retrospective. Remember learning and delivery are not separate activities.

- *A team member, either inadvertently or on purpose, continues to shift blame?*
  This situation presents a great opportunity to call for a break in the retrospective. Ask the team member to step aside (physically or virtually) for a private talk. Give the team member feedback on the impact of their behavior. If they need help, offer to meet with them to discuss it further. In the meantime, ask them to agree to stop blaming during the retrospective in progress. This usually works well. In the tiny percentage of cases when the team member will not agree, you have two options: One, announce that you are prematurely closing the retrospective. Two, explain that the retrospective is no longer a safe space and ask the team members how they'd like to proceed. After the retrospective, explore hidden or unresolved issues.
- *A team member truly messed up?*
  Return to Kerth's retrospective prime directive. Did the team member show up intending to "mess up" that day? It's unlikely. Judgment and blame are not helping this team member. They result in undermining a potentially valuable team member's further performance. How did the situation contribute to creating the opportunity for "mess"? What can be learned?

- *They don't attend the retrospective?*
  People do things for reasons. What might be their
  reason? Are meetings ineffective? Have you communicated the topic and outcome? Have you communicated
  their role and the benefit to participants? What is the
  risk if they don't attend? Have previously decided
  action items been ignored? People do not want to invest
  time in something that feels wasteful and pointless.
  Make your invitation transparent, clear, and sincere.

If they realize it's not a good match, set the expectation that
people may leave meetings. Despite discomfort, many people remain in meetings that have ceased to add value. This discomfort grows and carries into future meetings. The assumption
becomes that meetings are a waste of time. Increase autonomy
to increase value and participation.

Reflections for Your Learning

Begin accelerating the essential motivators today. Learning leaders focus intensely on resilient learning for the organization,
teams, and themselves.

How might more frequent and widespread retrospectives
shake up assumptions in your organization?

How have you seen the effectiveness and ineffectiveness of
leaders as learning facilitators?

How could you adapt the example to fit your organization? What similarities and differences would you
expose?

How do the Learning Leaders 4Cs (compassion, complexity, confidence, and courage) affect retrospectives?

PART TWO

The Resilience Factors

In Part Two, we introduce the *resilience factors*. Leadership through learning acknowledges the role of growing resilience to discover value. Learning leaders achieve results by enabling resilient learning teams. The essential motivators—purpose, co-intelligence, and autonomy—lay the foundation for enabling high performance. All three motivators are essential.

Purpose and autonomy without co-intelligence creates subpar quality.

Purpose and co-intelligence without autonomy equals dependencies and bottlenecks.

Co-intelligence and autonomy with no purpose means we do things for the sake of doing things.

All three are essential.

Yet, while essential, they may not be enough. Leaders go beyond the essential motivators to foster resilient learning teams. They address extra factors. These resilience factors are collaborative connection, inclusive collaboration, minimizing power dynamics, and embracing conflict. They are the underlying forces that either evolve teams or break teams during chaos. They are the secret sauce. When learning leaders focus on building resilience, the focus moves from blame and shame toward learning and growth.

In the following four chapters, we'll explore the four resilience factors. You can read them in any order, but learning leaders will need them all. In Chapter 6, we'll examine the realities of **collaborative connection**. In Chapter 7, we'll unlock the potential of **conflict** that boosts resiliency. In Chapter 8, we'll explore how to create **inclusive collaboration**. In Chapter 9, we'll unpack the **power dynamics** within teams. In these chapters, we'll provide retrospective examples. They focus on building both essential motivators and resilience factors.

Discovering the Resilience Factors

Leaders experience pride in helping a team become high performing. They also experience confusion and disappointment when a high-performing team breaks.

Soniya, an experienced director of education, felt proud of her history of leading a co-located administrative team. The team met all the definitions of high performance. They produced results. They collaborated. They didn't depend on Soniya for making all decisions. They enjoyed working together.

This high-performance team was no accident. Soniya had worked very hard to build a meaningful purpose for the team. They had stopped working as individuals and started working together. Soniya had increased the co-intelligence of the team through regular training and collaboration. Their growth mindset fostered a willingness to help outside their specializations. As the team focused on effective continuous learning, confidence increased. Soniya intentionally increased the areas in which the team made decisions directly. As the autonomy rose, their respon-

sibility for successful results exploded. Soniya and her team were rocking!

Then COVID-19 hit. As everyone began working from home, the team fell apart. Before Soniya could blink, they were acting like a group again. They were willing to help each other, but everyone wanted individual work assignments from her. Dates were missed. The quality of work dropped off. Blame and shame were rising. Soniya was completely confused. What happened to this high-performance team?

Soniya's team may have been high performing, but they didn't have resilience. Basically overnight, each person on the team faced similar and different challenges. The team still had a shared purpose. The team still had co-intelligence. The team still had autonomy. Yet delivery was now suffering.

When in unexpected conditions, maintaining high performance depends on the team's resilience. The resilience factors promote the team's ability to keep collaborative connections, their ability to be inclusive in their interactions, their ability to minimize power dynamics, and their ability to embrace conflict. These resilience factors evolve or break teams.

Introducing the Resilience Factors

As represented in the Leadership through Learning model (Figure P2.1), the four resilience factors are the secret sauce that builds upon the essential motivators.

The Collaborative Connection Resilience Factor

Ensure a psychologically safe environment through learning, trust, shared reflection, and connection. When people learn and deliver together, they collaboratively connect with one another.

Figure P2.1 Leadership through Learning

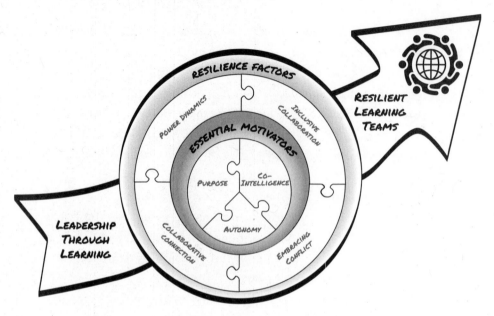

When people collaborate, they focus less on individual success or failure. Hence the shift away from blame and shame. When people connect as a team, trust helps the team deliver. These conditions encourage shared responsibility.

The Conflict Resilience Factor

Ensure that people can embrace conflict in healthy ways. Conflict is not only inevitable but vital in the workplace. Resilient learning teams take conflict as a sign that something is trying to happen. Conflict provides opportunities to benefit from and create co-intelligence from collective wisdom. How we choose to handle conflict determines whether we become stronger or more frail as a team. If we keep conflict healthy, there is no value from blame and shame.

The Inclusive Collaboration Resilience Factor

Ensure that all team members feel welcomed and feel that they belong. Ensure that everyone can engage fully and authentically, both in the decision-making processes and in learning opportunities. When everyone feels a sense of belonging, shame and blame are minimized. This factor fosters the potential for the biggest gains in results. Given the value of co-intelligence, people are lagging in creating inclusive collaborative environments.

The Power Dynamics Resilience Factor

Ensure that power is acknowledged, balanced, or minimized to create a level playing field for engagement. Organizational dynamics introduce formal and unspoken power. Teams encounter many forms of power dynamics. Power makes a difference in who gets heard, which ideas are followed, and who belongs. Power can support or, more often, get in the way of resilience. Understanding power dynamics fosters an increased openness. It lessens intentional or unintentional blame and mixed messages.

When Soniya's team was on-site together, there had been moments of tension. Yet they were always successful. They were able to focus on delivery with enough stability to obscure the team's lack of resiliency. But Soniya quickly learned that high-performance teams could fall apart. When unexpected events happened, the team's lack of resilience amplified their underlying issues. Suddenly, moments of tension became huge challenges without the resiliency to address them.

To enable the opportunity for business agility, delivery has to continue no matter what conditions prevail—even chaotic situations. The time had come for Soniya to be a learning leader.

Tony Lambert, vice president of client engineering, often reinforces resiliency. He reported that he coaches other leaders and team members to "flow like water, not stone. The strongest structures in nature are flexible structures. Teams that are able to flex, bend, expand, grow, and shrink are much more resilient and stronger than a static stone."[1]

Engaging collaborative connections means greater trust.

Building inclusive collaboration means greater wisdom.

Encouraging healthy conflict means greater creativity.

Being transparent about power dynamics means greater engagement.

Taken together, all four produce resilient teams.

CHAPTER 6

The Collaborative Connection Resilience Factor

Everyone wants a trustworthy team. Learning leaders want confidence in the team's ability to make decisions and deliver outcomes. Yet equally important is for the team to trust leadership to create resilient learning teams, nurture trust, and reinforce connections.

At an education company, a rollout of a new training was important. A leader notified a team that he felt they were empowered to take on this task. The team trusted this decree. The only upfront request was that the team give a plan update at the end of the week. That seemed reasonable.

The team worked many hours considering the needs, dependencies, and risks. They were super excited to meet with the leader to share their plan. In the meeting, the leader proceeded to rip apart the plan and veto several team decisions. At that moment, the team accepted every change without discussion. The team members walked out of the meeting completely demoralized and angry. They quickly realized that they were not empowered.

During the next several weekly meetings, the leader noticed a difference in interactions. In each discussion, the team deferred to the leader for decisions. The leader was confused about why team members seemed not to care anymore.

This is an all too common story. The argument on behalf of the leader for why the veto was necessary sounds like, "But I can't let them make bad decisions! I helped the team!" The leader assumed the team would view the changes as a learning opportunity. But the "trust but verify" style of leadership rarely achieves quality results, because there is rarely trust involved. So teams never take responsibility. The veto changes created a sense of distrust and a "we have been set up" experience. Without any recognition of the broken trust, responsibility transferred back to the leader.

No leader or organization can build enough trust in one shot, overnight. It takes time, persistence, and a dedicated understanding of the benefits. Small yet frequent collaborative activities provide opportunities. Building trust to build connections is not linear or one-directional. The interactions you choose can take steps forward or backward. This leader's approach had broken trust and had lingering negative impacts. We are not recommending that this leader do a trust-fall activity to begin rebuilding trust. Try the following activity instead.

Motivation, Trust, and Safety Activity

For the first time, allow up to 30 minutes.[1] As people understand how it works, you can reuse it more quickly later. If your group is meeting in person, you can set this up with a whiteboard or flip chart. If meeting virtually, you can use an online whiteboard tool.

1. Create a five-row-by-six-column grid (Table 6.1). Title the grid "Motivation and Safety: How Prepared Are We to Do This Work Together?" Label the row dimensions as motivation and the column dimensions as safety (this is optional).

Table 6.1 Motivation, Trust, and Safety Activity

Motivation and safety grid	5: I'll agree with whatever is said and keep my real thoughts to myself.	4: I'm not going to say much and will hope that others bring up all the issues.	3: I will talk about some things and keep others to myself.	2: I will discuss most things.	1: I will talk openly about anything.
A. I really want to learn from our successes and setbacks.					
B. I'd like to see whether there is something in this for me.					
C. I appreciate the chance to be away from our usual work.					
D. I have to be here but I'd rather be anywhere else instead.					

2. Give each row a title and letter, starting at the bottom with D and moving upward to A at the top. These indicate an increasing willingness to engage and seek solutions.

3. Give each column a number and a title, starting at the left column with 5 and moving to the rightmost with 1. These are descriptions of an increasing sense of psychological safety and willingness to be honest and vulnerable.

4. Collect the data anonymously. Place responses in the corresponding cells on the grid. Acknowledge that no answer is good or bad. Everyone gains by having a clear idea about the perspectives and degree of trust present.

5. Ask the following three questions and pause after each for response and discussion, as needed. Again, accept all responses as valid.
   a. What do you see on the grid?
   b. How ready is the team to work? (If they think they are ready, stop here and move on with the agenda. If they don't think they are ready, ask the next question.)
   c. What would it take to get ready?

6. If the team is not ready to work, decide which next step to take. Follow this with an exercise of creating one or more ground rules that help improve trust and safety. Follow this with another vote to ensure that you have everyone's buy-in for moving forward.

In the next weekly meeting, the leader used the motivation, trust, and safety activity. This activity opened a discussion regarding the impact of the leader's behaviors. And the leader acknowledged his desire to learn and grow.

*An opportunity presented itself quickly to try the new ground
rules. HR announced an initiative to enhance the onboarding
process. Again, the leader notified the team that they were
empowered. Unlike the last time, the leader clarified with more
details and boundaries to build autonomy. He noted specific
decisions that needed input before finalizing them and explained
why. To build co-intelligence, the leader arranged training on key
HR elements required. He examined risks for potential vetoes
and collaboratively created risk responses. This change in approach gave the team the ability to achieve the purpose.*

With each of these interactions, better connections formed.
The leader had confidence in the team's skills and knowledge,
and the team gained trust in the leader's intentions for their success. Over time, the leader was able to expand the team's trust
and true empowerment. Increasing a sense of team cohesion, investment, and connections builds resiliency.

The Law of Decadigitality

Quick challenge: say that ten times fast!

Forming connections takes into account the number of people
involved. The best collaboration means full engagement through
trusting and trustworthy connections. Yet there's a balance to
strike. Each engaged team member adds to gaining skills, perspectives, and commitments for co-intelligence. But it also means
more complications for communication, collaboration, and decision making.

*An internal organization service team had responsibilities that
spanned numerous areas. Over the years, this team became the
catch-all for projects that didn't have dedicated owners.*

As responsibilities grew, the team size grew. They were now up to 24 people. The team was struggling and overwhelmed with the volume and variety of the workload. The original work approach was to have each person own one of the projects. But now, this solution was creating new problems. Projects were falling through the cracks because they were waiting on one individual. The team was constantly in reactive mode.

One of the team members, Kim, decided something had to change. She was exhausted, and so was the rest of the team. Kim initiated a retrospective for the team. In the retrospective, people were able to acknowledge the root challenges. The team discussed the pros and cons of optimal team sizes. After a lengthy discussion, they arrived at an experiment. The team would break into four new subteams, or, as they called them, ranger teams. Each team requested a set of projects that they were to focus on together. They decided to test it out immediately. They broke into the four ranger teams to determine their next steps. It typically took several hours to arrive at decisions, but now it happened in 60 minutes. More importantly, people felt focused, aligned, heard, and connected.

Learning leaders focus on ensuring that everyone hears each voice. Every extra person contributes a single new connection point with each possible combination. Agile coach George Dinwiddie has a sense of humor we value. He contributed the law of decadigitality. Dinwiddie says, "Team communication difficulty increases in direct proportion to the number of ten toes involved in the conversation."[2] The number of sets of toes in communication has enormous implications for everyone. This is expressed in the communication connection chart in Figure 6.1.

It is easier to manage the dynamics of a 6-person team than those of a 10-person team. Moreover, it will be even easier than a 15-person team. Clinical psychologist Emily Anhalt commented on the chart in Figure 6.1: "Every combination of people in a group

Figure 6.1 Lines of Communication Nodes

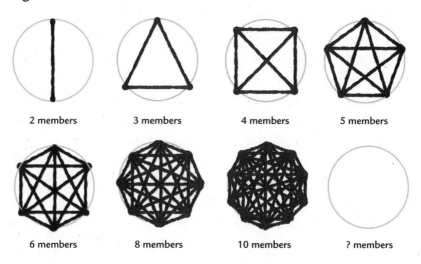

2 members	3 members	4 members	5 members
6 members	8 members	10 members	? members

Lines of communication
with increasing number of nodes (i.e., team members).
How many are on your team?

contributes to the greater dynamic. For a group to be healthy, it should bond as a whole, but also nurture individual relationships within itself."[3] People bring more than an inert node to the team. Learning leaders have confidence that each team member provides and receives information in a variety of ways that bring value.

Learning leaders show compassion for the challenges of connecting different perspectives. They design spaces using techniques to foster and embrace various approaches of thinking and engagement, because they know that if anyone feels ignored or unable to understand information, collaboration breaks.

The larger the team, the more the connections become difficult to manage. Learning leaders model and respect the complexity of increasing connections. When advocating for manageable team sizes, learning leaders courageously make space for resiliency.

Words of advice:

- People need time to collect their thoughts before engaging with others. First provide time for individual thinking. Then follow with various small-group and larger-group discussions. As team size increases, designs need more time allocated. Instructions, discussions, and decisions all take longer to engage everyone.
- Provide techniques for queued participation—for example, stacked ordering of questions via hand raising or putting a request in the chat.
- Keep group discussions between two and eight people. For virtual interactions, keep group discussions between three and six people. The smaller the number, the more opportunities people have to engage. For virtual interactions, a lot of time can be wasted with pair breakouts. For example, someone's computer freezes or they get called away right at that moment. In a room, a quick adjustment of pairing is easy. Virtually, this can expend a lot of time and create frustration.
- With eight or more participants in an event, be intentional about when you rotate breakout groups. Consider safety requests for people who do not want to switch spots (virtual or physical). For example, offer a request of at least two people to rotate to a new group. This provides freedom to those who have a seat or breakout group preference. It also offers opportunities for those who want to engage with fresh viewpoints. There are also times when keeping the same breakout assignments is important. For example, during a vulnerable multistep discussion on safety, keep the groups stable.

Making the Connection

Support team members to come together to create a cohesive, connected feeling. A right-sized team of professionals may build trust and strong working relationships. But achieving "team-i-ness" and resiliency doesn't happen automatically. Learning leaders create the conditions for connections to develop—for example, through team chartering.

From the beginning, team chartering sets the tone for trust and connection for the team—and for the approach to the work. In *Liftoff: Start and Sustain Successful Agile Teams*, Diana Larsen and Ainsley Nies describe a template for team chartering.[4] They highlight three elements for team identity and the path to success: purpose, alignment, and context. Each element has three aspects:

- To clarify the drivers for the team's purpose: Vision for their product or service, team mission or approach to accomplishing the work, and mission tests or success indicators
- To form the heart of alignment: Simple rules, core team characteristics, and working agreements
- To identify the external connections in the context: Boundaries, interactions, and committed resources

Purpose, alignment, and context have a strong parallel with the essential motivators. Chartering the team establishes an understanding among team members and leaders. It clarifies their purpose, autonomy, and expectations for co-intelligence.

James, director of mobile engineering, had an epiphany. Discrete individuals working in isolation have failed to meet deadlines. He thought forming cross-functional teams might work better. But he needed to tap into his connections with other leaders to try this experiment. After securing the approvals, he'd put together business analysts, programmers, testers, designers, and user experience specialists.

James wanted the teams to have a chance to make a meaningful impact on business outcomes. So he advocated for the pilot teams to have products with substantial weight. A group of leaders decided on a new product that would integrate with a product requiring critical upgrades.

James combined volunteers with a few invited employees to form three pilot teams. The products selected meant these teams would need to collaborate. Most team members were eager for the experiment, but others joined as skeptics. He wondered how he could get everyone on board for an effort they could all support.

Then James attended a conference. He learned about liftoffs and team chartering. He thought he'd try a joint chartering session as a way to initiate the effort.

Luckily, a team of facilitators were available within the organization. A facilitator consulted with an external coach to gain competence on team chartering. Then they designed the session, including prework for James and other leaders to develop the draft product visions for all three teams.

James and other leaders participated at the start of the chartering session. They disclosed the intent and purpose of the pilot experiment with cross-functional teams, explaining that they sought a more effective way to produce products. They hypothesized that cross-functional teams might be the best approach. They wanted to model and select people for the teams who were willing to experiment. At the same time, the outcomes would play a role in determining the future direction of the business. This was not a trivial venture!

The facilitators spent a day and a half with the three teams. To clarify the drivers for the teams' purpose, they started by introducing the rough draft of the product visions. Then the team collaborated with leaders on evolving this into a workable first draft. Upon this success, the facilitators completed additional purpose activities. Then they continued to move the team through their activities for alignment and context. At the end, every team had a first draft of a team charter. Over time, they could continue to tune and improve their team charters to fit each team and its work.

Team chartering met James's goal of getting everyone on board for an effort they could all support. Team members knew why the leaders brought them together. They now shared a meaningful purpose. Team members understood the criticality of their product and how it would contribute to business direction. Teams had autonomy and agreed on how they would approach the work. They explored how they would work with others in the organization. They had begun building co-intelligence. They practiced resilient learning skills they would need.

James and the other leaders were eager to see how the experiment would progress. They saw that bringing everyone together for a focused start had accelerated performance. Team members continued to build on the connections fostered in team chartering, leading to collaboration that decreased time to deployment. The teams were able to produce their deliverable in half the time that it would have taken if they were integrating individually assigned work. And with shared responsibility, they experienced less blame and shame in the team. Leaders began thinking about other work that might benefit from team chartering.

As James received new inquiries about team chartering, he replied, "I've seen the power of tapping into the 'wisdom of the crowd' to plan the work. It's not about creating a static document. Team chartering is about setting the conditions for the right connections to happen, for trust building to begin and team members to commit to the effort. What matters is taking the time for team chartering. It's an investment."

"To help a team self-organize, just put them in a room together and lock the door." A consultant, who will remain nameless, gave this bad advice. Refer back to the five rules of learning. Remember the leader has a role in creating the setting for continuous learning. Team chartering establishes the leader's intent to start with trust and connection. It works in many dimensions—between and among team members, between the team and its organizational partners, between the team and its customers, and, perhaps most critically, between leaders and teams.

Words of advice:

- Some teams don't start their work together with chartering. Other teams forget to iterate on their team charter. If so, all is not lost. Use chartering for team "restarts" when a team gets off course or finds itself thrashing. Or when a team gains or loses so many members it needs to start over. Or they learn more about the work and, working together, revise part, or all, of their team charter.
- While chartering, practice effective listening. Are you listening to learn or listening to respond?[5]
- Select a facilitator with strong group process skills. Facilitators require the ability to improvise activities to engage all the voices. And remember, facilitators remain neutral. The content in a team charter must be created by the team, not the facilitator.[6]
- Set aside time for chartering for teams of leaders too. Bring your peers together to reinforce leadership efforts. The best organizational change efforts evolve when leaders form into teams. Leadership teams understand their collective role in transitioning to meet new circumstances. For example, consider a team of senior sales managers. Before, they had siloed functional responsibili-

ties for different sizes and types of customers. Customers were frustrated with trying to buy but having to speak to several people before finding one who was "allowed" to sell to them. The leaders realized they had to develop a collaborative approach to quickly satisfy customers. The leaders were planning to implement a large change to the sales department. They needed to understand their own purpose, develop their own aligned work process, and lead within their business context as leaders together.

Tuning the Connection

Resilient learning teams do not instantly become resilient. Nor are they guaranteed to remain resilient. Keeping collaborative connections resilient requires frequent tuning.

Connections need more healthy interactions and fewer destructive interactions. A healthy relationship state needs five supportive interactions for every negative interaction.[7] This ratio helps people's capacity to process negative interactions in a constructive way. People can become complacent about investing energy into connections and trust. They fall into the trap of "This is so much better. We don't need any of that anymore." It can be tempting to just tell the team what their problem is. But learning learners know that approach doesn't promote responsibility. Instead, information radiators offer a critical tool that learning leaders use to increase transparency.

> *Information radiator* is the generic term for any number of visible written, drawn, printed, or electronic displays. All team members, as well as passers-by, can see the latest information at a glance. A radiator conveys key information. Use it to visualize the flow of work. It shows where bottlenecks occur and enables anyone to see what the team is working on at any time.[8]

A team struggled with balancing the workload for sunsetting a product. The senior team members complained to their leader, Tricia. In the past, Tricia's instinct would have been to reassign tasks to different people. But this would damage the team's autonomy. Or worse, it would demonstrate a lack of compassion and single people out for not taking on enough. Now Tricia was trying to be a learning leader. So during a retrospective, she leveraged information radiators to shine a spotlight on the problem. On the wall, she depicted the workload of the team over the past three months.

When learning leaders display information radiators, they should remain focused on learning. Otherwise, they run the risk of damaging trust and connections. If Tricia displayed weaponized metrics, the team's trust would suffer damage—for example, if she produced a report with a single number indicating "completed items per person." If she followed this with publicly rewarding the "winners," more problems would occur. The connections would break, hindering further conversations. Tricia's information radiator was a graph containing a card for every task per team member in the upcoming work.

Tricia expected that some individuals might say, "Wow. We will do more!" But after displaying the visual, Tricia remained silent. Then something surprising happened. A team member looked directly at the two senior team members and offered, "Will you both please let us do something? We want to help!"

With a little more conversation, everyone learned that the senior members thought they were faster. They picked up tasks before others could volunteer. Until they saw it clearly represented on the wall, they overlooked the root problem. The visual allowed the team to discuss the issue as a whole. Whereas before, the focus was on individuals not helping, by the end of the discussion, trust and connections were rebuilding.

Leadership through learning means having the courage to increase transparency without blame. A learning leader enables and has confidence in their team to tune themselves. The visual cues anchor the team's attention. It fosters people building and collaborating on each other's ideas. They are able to compassionately see and learn what others recognize or experience. They build an awareness of complexity within the bigger picture. All this leads to a sense of shared responsibility and resiliency.

Tuning the team is about continuously learning and evolving together.

Words of advice:

- Be selective about how many information radiators are provided. Avoid overwhelming the team with so much information that they can't take a step together. Focus on what problems need a spotlight. Focus on those that are causing significant impacts. Focus on where team members highlight challenges they want resolved.
- Use sets of information radiators. Share relevant sets of data metrics to find trends and provide a systems view of the issues. Avoid highlighting individual accomplishments or failures.
- Ask key questions to help minimize weaponized use of metrics. How is this metric informing the team? How can this metric be manipulated? Can this metric guide the team on a successful path toward achieving their purpose?
- Rely on an information radiator only as long as it provides fresh insights. Information radiators that hang around too long become overly familiar and unnoticed. They add unwanted visual noise to the

team's work environment. When would we stop using this metric?

- Encourage the team to tune the connections based on their positive accomplishments. When teams intensely focus on growing, improving, and changing, they may experience burnout. Stretch into growth experiences, then also provide time for integrating, reflection, and fun. Teams that celebrate together focus on highlighting the positives to encourage, tune, and sustain connections. Celebration doesn't always need to be elaborate gestures. A quick yet personal appreciation note is very powerful and motivating.

Example Design

Learning leaders encourage their teams to become resilient learning teams by highlighting underlying challenges, not once but continuously along the way. They invite the team to use a retrospective to explore specific topics. As a leader, you don't get to decide what the team's outcome action items are. Yet you can choose to focus on the area where you've observed that the team is struggling. The retrospective example given here showcases how leaders encourage collaborative connection guided by the Retrospectives for Resilience (Figure 6.2). Note that this is not the only retrospective design for this specific topic.

Scenario

Remember the story from Chapter 1 about John, whose lack of participation in retrospectives was legendary among his peers (see the "Learning Leaders 4Cs" section). This was the design that got a compliment from him.

Figure 6.2 Retrospectives for Resilience

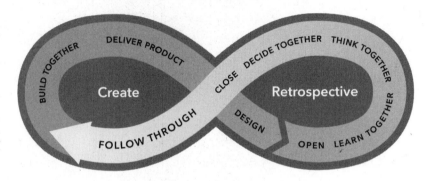

Retrospective Logistics

- **Facilitator intent:** Logistics influence the *setting* to ensure that it supports the team's learning
- **Setting:** In person
- **Number of participants:** Invited 28
- **Duration:** Half day (1:00–5:00 p.m.), with lunch provided beforehand (12:00–1:00 p.m.)
- **Day:** Thursday
- **Food:** Lunch, water, soda, afternoon snacks
- **Location:** On-site large conference room
- **Setup:** One U-shaped table set up with room around the table for small-group activities; accessory table for supplies, including flip charts, markers, sticky notes, and so on.

Retrospective Design

The retrospective design provides a process outline for the facilitator to accomplish the goal.

Set the Stage (20 Minutes)

- **Facilitator intent:** To help everyone participate at the start of the retrospective and to build shared experience and trust (*collaborative connection*). To align on the topic or outcome. To encourage learning, collaboration, and creativity (*alive*). To model and set the tone for blame-free engagement and increase safety. To keep the team's *purpose obvious* by focusing on real work (*fluency*) aspects right from the beginning.
- **Overall retrospective agenda**
- **Topic:** Greater sales momentum for XProduct.
- **Outcome:** Define two to four actions that will help the sales team sell more XProduct.
- **Activity:** Collaborative drawing exercise.[9] In groups of up to five people, the first person has a blank sheet of paper and a writing utensil. The first person will think of an animal that represents XProduct, then draw one line of that animal without sharing what animal they selected. Then the paper is passed clockwise, with the second person adding the next line to make an animal. Continue passing until an animal is recognized. Then discuss as a group what the originally intended animal was versus the animal drawn. How is the emergent collaborative animal a better representation of XProduct? How did trust show up in this activity?

Gather Data (45 Minutes)

- **Facilitator intent:** To create safety for exploring this topic with choice on individual contributions (*autonomy*). To use small groups to focus collaboratively on examining the data (*collaborative connection*). To increase visibility, internalization, and normalization of the data being shared (*fluency*). Pulling each team member's perspective on the work so far makes the whole team experience more *obvious* to everyone and builds the momentum of *co-intelligence*.

- **Data:** Display sales metrics including new customer acquisition, customer retention, upsell trends, and so on. Share a visual summary of their workflow. Provide the list of prioritized sales strategies.
- **Activity:** Shout out what immediately jumps out at you.[10]
- **Activity:** Highlight that learning can be challenging, as we have to slow down to speed up, so we need lots of ideas. In triads, discuss the bottlenecks and issues the group identifies. Have a volunteer from the group share the top two on sticky notes and verbally with everyone. For duplicates, put the notes together on the board.

Break (10 Minutes)

- **Facilitator intent:** Attending to team members' physical and mental needs helps them stay energized and refreshed (*alive*) for the work.
- Encourage healthy choices such as beverages, a quick walk, and so on.

Generate Insights (75 Minutes)

- **Facilitator intent:** To foster shared responsibility by allowing space for individual thought, collaborative interactions, creative exploration, varied opinions, and acknowledgment of the complexity. Encourage all voices and respectful examination of ideas, impacts, implications, and challenges (*collaborative connection*). Explore the feasibility of new insights and experiments emerging (*co-intelligence*). Staying focused with targeted questions helps momentum (*obvious*). Gathering insights relies on collaborative learning, analysis, internalization, and identification of options (fluency and *co-intelligence*). Build upon individual voices toward a shared collaborative discussion (*collaborative connection*).

- **Activity (15 minutes):** For 2 minutes, silently consider, "When you look at these issues, what connections or relationships exist between them?" Two groups of the previous triads join together to form a group of six. Have each group discuss what observations each person had.

- **Activity (50 minutes):** Introduce the "yes, and" mindset and adapt the 1-2-4-All liberating structure.[11] Individually, each participant puts on a single sticky note (kept with them) an experiment to countermeasure one of the issues noted. After a minute, each participant finds a new person they have not been in a group with. Have the groups discuss each idea and look for pros or cons and opportunities to build on current ideas (yes, and). Each pair determines the best countermeasure to put forth jointly. As a pair, they join with another pair (ideally, again, people they have not worked with yet today). Again, have the groups discuss both ideas and look for pros or cons and opportunities to build on current ideas. Have each group of four determine the best countermeasure to put forth jointly. Each of the seven groups' volunteers will enter a queue to share their selected countermeasure with everyone and display it on a large board.

Break (10 Minutes)

- **Facilitator intent:** Attending to team members' physical and mental needs helps them stay energized and refreshed (*alive*) for the work.
- Encourage healthy choices such as beverages, a quick walk, and so on.

Decide What to Do (50 Minutes)

- **Facilitator intent:** Ideally to converge on the two to four action items that have the most energy and interest (*alive*). Bring the team together to decide the action items to improve the work (*fluency*) that everyone can support (*purpose* and *autonomy*). With equal voices and volunteering, encourage *collaborative connection*.

- **Activity:** Each participant writes down their first, second, and third choices on a sticky note. Everyone stands next to their first-choice countermeasure. Remove countermeasures with zero to three individuals standing near them. If more than four countermeasures remain, the individuals next to the one with the fewest votes must select a second choice from what options remain.

- **Activity:** Each countermeasure group will form a hypothesis of what the countermeasure results could be.[12] A volunteer shares with everyone the hypothesis. Based on reactions, return to the group and update accordingly. In addition, define an experiment to test the hypothesis. For example, a hypothesis is, "If we eliminate the extra approval for pricing of groups under 50, more small companies will become customers." An example test is, "For one cohort there will be no approval step, and for the other cohorts the approval step will remain. Collect data and compare." Clearly, other factors can contribute. Ideally, the use of multiple tests helps reduce the variables. Discuss roles required, timelines, and so on for this countermeasure. Then two volunteers who will represent this countermeasure share the plan for being transparent about the progress.

Close the Retrospective (15 Minutes)

- **Facilitator intent:** To intentionally take time to acknowledge others and reinforce the specific positive aspects of working together collaboratively through the problems to solve (*alive*). To reinforce effective work relationships (*collaborative connection*). To gather feedback for the facilitator to use for future retrospectives.
- **Communicate location of transparency updates**
- **Activity:** If desired, each individual can post a high dream (a deepest, desired goal) sticky note for the next retrospective.[13]
- **Activity:** If desired, share any high dreams for XProduct sales.

  Note: This retrospective event was scheduled for four hours. The design accounts for 3 hours and 45 minutes. The additional 15 minutes is buffer time for unexpected adjustments to the design. For example, the group may need more time for a discussion than was planned.

Tricia included several elements to build connections for sustaining a resilient learning team. The *flow* of activities orchestrated gradual attention to trust and collaboration (*collaborative connection*) in order to build toward the outcome. She immediately set the engagement tone by *courageously* exploring the power of collaboration. She included small-group activities to give space for people to be heard and engage based on their preferences (*collaborative connection*). She expressed *confidence* in the team's ability to move forward together. She provided people with opportunities to highlight *complexity* in their decisions. She ended by celebrating the potential of what this team can accomplish.

Retrospectives offer one tangible way to build connections. They provide a container for the reinforcement of learning, collaboration, engagement, and trust. The reflecting, examining, creating, and deciding on experiments together fosters improvement. This unlocks more potential for improving together. The team develops an understanding of their mutual willingness and *responsibility* to deliver. All this builds resiliency in the team.

But What If . . . ?

- *Team members refuse to engage in "collaborative connection" activities—the same people participate and the same people don't?*
  Examine the work setting. Choose activities that encourage participants to build compassion for each other and compassion for the difficulty of the situation. Choose invitation over mandatory participation. Express the value of their participation. Keep reminding people that meetings are real work and learning is not a separate activity. Cultivate honest, inclusive, and trustworthy engagement in every meeting, not only retrospectives.

  The words "team building" make some people nervous. Few people want kumbaya exercises in the workplace. And unfortunately, that association exists even if they are not the same thing. Start with engaging in difficult work topics associated with trust and psychological safety. There may even be small adjustments that would dramatically change someone's engagement. Adjust designs for more autonomy in participation, aligning with team members' styles. Or simply let them observe the activity. Engage them with what they noticed. Then model and express commitment to the benefits of continuous team learning. To achieve co-intelligence, trust and connection must exist.

- *Other leaders want to dictate what is in the team charter?*
  Try to remember that rarely are leaders trying to break
  trust, cause delays, and so on. Take the time to explain the
  value of the team's responsibility in determining their
  own team charter. Express the benefits for the team,
  leadership, organization, and customers. Clarify the parts
  of the charter (product vision) that leaders control. Other
  parts of the charter cover the team's work process and
  stay within the team's autonomy. All may need collaborative discussion. Reiterate that teams may want to
  consult with leaders as they learn more and their draft
  charter needs updating. Hold the line against dictating,
  courageously!

- *Team members balk when discovering new information that*
  changes priorities for action?
  Action items may need resizing. Break down items into
  smaller steps. Expect that discoveries and changes may
  happen. Make it transparent. In complex products,
  expect and leave openings for discovery. Shifting
  priorities can be disconcerting and demoralizing if a lot
  of work has gone down the "wrong" path. Reluctance
  to change priorities doesn't necessarily signal disengagement. Make complexities clear by demonstrating
  the need for flexibility.[14]

- *I still don't trust my teammates?*
  Trust can go missing for many reasons. You may have
  had experiences with people on your team that show
  they are not worthy of your trust. You may have had
  experiences in the past of untrustworthy teammates.
  Or you may have heard gossip about the current team
  and judged. Look for the reasons that trust is missing.
  Once you understand the root, you will be able to
  identify your options—for example, adopting transpar-

ency by openly bringing up team issues in a retrospective, or even accepting that the time has come to find a different team. Consider all the options before deciding.

Reflections for Your Learning

Begin building the collaborative connection resilience factor today. Learning leaders focus intensely on resilient learning for the organization, teams, and themselves.

How healthy are trust and connections in your organization?

How are you helping teams and team members make connections?

How is team size (i.e., the law of decadigitality) affecting your team's trust and connection?

Which teams would benefit from a team chartering session?

How have you helped the team tune themselves?

How could you adapt the example to fit your organization? What similarities and differences would you expose?

How do the Learning Leaders 4Cs (compassion, complexity, confidence, and courage) affect connections?

CHAPTER 7

The Conflict Resilience Factor

C onflict scares many people. When people think of conflict, they conjure thoughts of personal attacks and arguments. Yet engaging in conflict is not only inevitable but vital in the workplace. If we say wisdom of the crowd is essential, this means conflict will happen in order for the best results to emerge. Conflict is a sign that something is trying to happen and that we have differing ideas about how to help it along. How we choose to handle conflict determines whether we evolve or break as a team.

Diana's Team Communication Model depicts the inherent elements of healthy communication in teams (Figure 7.1).[1] Healthy communication fosters productive connections as well. Every connection begins with creating enough trust to agree to engage in the work. Team interactions and collaboration emerge from a foundation of trust.

Trust: Team trust incorporates each team member's willingness to extend trust to others and to act in a trustworthy way themselves. Trust must flow two ways. At work, it relies on three aspects: credibility, support, and consistency. Credibility comes when others see us as capable and competent in our role and feel that our word is believable. Support emerges when others perceive our willingness to express mutual respect and civility, as well as when we show interest in the lives of others and share what is important in our own lives. Consistency gives others the sense that we will show up reliably and dependably. All three aspects together assert our personal character and competence as trust-

Figure 7.1 Team Communication Model

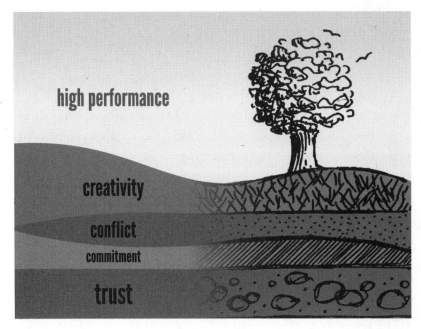

worthy and convey that we behave according to our values and beliefs.

Commitment: With enough starting trust, we begin to explore our collective commitment. Commitment shows itself in three ways: commitment to the value of the work, commitment to team health, and commitment to each team member's well-being. As we show the reality of our commitments, it adds to the trust in the team. Greater trust strengthens commitment. Thus, we begin a virtuous spiral through the layers of the model. Each layer builds on and contributes to the ones that came before.

Conflict: Embrace and grow a healthy, constructive approach to conflict. This is made possible through the grounding of being able to rely on each other's trust and commitment. Conflict is working through different ideas or approaches toward a shared goal. Conflict may remain uncomfortable, but it is no longer threatening. When each conflict is worked through together, this continues to reinforce trust and commitment.

Creativity: When our team can handle conflict, we unlock a new ability. Now we can innovate and be creative together. We can build on each other's ideas and find ways toward greater improvements. The unleashed creativity happens once we acknowledge that no one individual can think of everything. Collaborative creativity strengthens our resolve to address conflict, deepens the commitment, and further bolsters our trust.

High performance: All these interactions and foci of communication merge to create synergy. The collective team's energy gives higher-quality results. Remaining at this level depends on the ability to handle team conflicts and keep communication open. If all resilience factors are being proactively addressed, this state includes team resiliency.

A team's communication depends on the ability to recognize, confront, and collaborate through conflicts. As we work together, conflicts inevitably arise. Teams have a choice to avoid conflict, which often only increases the frequency and intensity of future conflict. Or teams can develop confidence and co-intelligence in their conflict capabilities. Resilient learning teams rely on the ability to learn their way through differences of opinion and through unknown, unexpected, and ambiguous conflicts.

A new team of program administrators planned a series of 90-minute retrospectives. They expected they would individually work on tasks much of the time. Yet, occasionally, some team members would collaborate on program policies and procedures. The facilitator knew that establishing a basis of trust among the team was a priority. This would help their cooperative and collaborative interactions. They spent much of the first retrospective reviewing previous programs and gaining more clarity about each other's approaches to work. During a connection activity,

*each person shared information about themselves on a visual
graphic of a shield. As each person presented their own shield,
team members saw different presentation styles. They learned
information about each other's backgrounds and preparation for
their roles. They learned about each person's learning goals. They
closed the retrospective by choosing a few working agreements.
One was, "We work best together when we check in on our shared
Slack space at least once per day and share highlights."*

*In the next retrospective three weeks later, they each shared
about the business outcomes of the programs. The director of
programs had accepted an invitation to this retrospective. As they
shared, they could ask the director of programs questions about
unclear areas. This clarified how these programs would contribute
to business direction and customer value. They came to agree on
their shared purpose. As a sign of public commitment, each person
signed a team purpose poster. Then each person finished the
sentence, "What I need to do my best work is . . ." This led to
updating the draft working agreement: "We work best together
when we keep our agreements, or if we can't, we tell teammates
of problems as soon as possible. We tell everyone through Slack.
And we communicate directly to those who will be most affected."*

*They spent the next two retrospectives going over the progress
they had made so far. The chosen improvement outcomes were
successful. They had standardized the forms for reporting. They
chose a few vital communication tools. For each discussion, they
encountered minor disagreements but easily worked through them.*

*In the next retrospective, they had a difficult outcome choice to
make. The topic was deciding how to interview their internal
customers. They had discussed three different ways of approaching
their internal customers. They were seeking a single standard
process they could all feel comfortable using. This choice was
blocking their next milestone. They entered the retrospective
nervous about losing the momentum they had created together.*

But they knew consistency would translate into co-intelligence in their team. Yet each had come to the program administration team with a strong preference for their own prior process. They thought their way was best and advocated for its adoption. Conflict was rising. As a first step, the facilitator reminded the team of their commitment to the shared purpose. They all wanted to create the best possible program outcome for their customers.

With this reminder, the team refocused. Team members found it easier to let go of their personal preferences in service of the goal. They began sorting through the similarities and differences. They looked for the things they liked best about other approaches. This helped remind the team of their trust in each other's capabilities. Eventually, they began collaborating on a new approach. They retained many of the best aspects from the various approaches. And new ideas emerged that excited them. They developed a shared interview style that no one had used before and that everyone thought would work well. They chose an experiment of using the new approach with a few customers, then reviewing the approach at the next retrospective. They would then decide whether to keep it or revise it for further experimentation.

Even as conflicts happened, this program administration team was able to communicate and collaborate by focusing on their foundation of trust and commitment. Over time, they became more creative and continued their growth toward resiliency. But no one said it was a smooth journey. Conflict is hard.

Behavior Challenges

Challenges inevitably arise with cooperative and collaborative work. The framing of conflict challenges frequently has a similar structure: How do I <stop, manage, address, etc.> <person(s)> from <negative behavior(s)>?

People seek resolutions that address the issue specifically with the problem person. But that is based on an assumption that the individual displaying this behavior is the problem. Learning leaders start with a focus on the setting that enables the behavior to occur.

For example, an influential team member may get labeled "bossy." They speak way too much and make all the decisions in the retrospective. A common reaction is to call this person a "jerk" and gossip about their control issues. What if they hate inefficient meetings and think they are helping by moving things along? When we only interact with critiques about their behavior, we limit the learning opportunities.

An operations director asked an HR leader, Lin, for feedback. The director expressed concerns about his operational managers. He was upset with their lack of engagement. Lin spoke with the six operational managers. They all mentioned their discomfort with the new director. They called him "a typical pointy-haired boss." To them, he seemed detached and only out for his own career, not for the good of the department or the company.

Trying to understand the bigger system, Lin dug deeper. The director role had recently been created as a condition of funding by a major investor. He'd been hired only a few months before. Previously, the operation managers reported directly to the vice president of operations. Now the director reported to the vice president. In the managers' perspectives, the director intentionally blocked their connection to decision makers. Lin heard that the director made decisions that overrode what the teams needed. The operational managers thought he was blocking progress, and started limiting interactions to reduce frustration. From the director's perspective, he was doing his job. He believed he didn't need to understand the past; he was supposed to create a new, higher-performing future. He was trying to make progress.

Also, Lin learned that the director was rarely present. Three weeks after his onboarding, the director was pulled away to deal with family issues. When he came back, he was quickly pulled away again, this time for an off-site quarterly reporting session with the investors. This was followed by his accompanying the directors of product and sales to several key customer meetings. Yet he knew that if he didn't get quick results, he could lose his job and the company could lose funding. To keep things moving, he had to make a few fast decisions.

Lin perceived how each individual saw the problem from the perspective of their own needs. Yet it was a systemic issue. Changes had occurred in their work system. They couldn't go back to the old way, but they hadn't yet discovered a new, more effective way to work as a team. They were stuck in the middle of this change, and they needed to learn their way out.

When Lin gave an overview of her observations to the director, he was stunned. He hadn't seen the patterns or their implications. The director knew they had to step back to move forward. He apologized to his team for his part in this mess. He made time to connect with each manager. He began to push back on the travel and meeting invitations to make sure he was present for essential events. He convened the management team to discuss their intentions for actions when he had to be away. They created a team charter together to build commitment. This included openly discussing how they wanted to work together through conflicts.

By acknowledging the complex systemic view, the director courageously took responsibility for his own behaviors that had caused distrust. He had contributed to the interaction norms that now frustrated him. His fears about job safety were increasing the conflict. His good intentions for progress didn't align with the impact on the team. The director was stuck in obligation and justified his behavior while judging theirs. He was not being compassionate. This was a no-win situation for everyone.

Building better connections from trust and commitment put this team on a path to shared responsibility. After everyone consistently improved their behaviors, a new and different team emerged. The director gained confidence in their abilities and engagement. Everyone became ready to embrace conflict.

Anyone is capable of bad behaviors, knowingly or unknowingly. Anyone is capable of not realizing the full impact of bad behaviors. Anyone is capable of justifying bad behaviors. And anyone is capable of learning. Learning leaders create opportunities for others to build complexity awareness of how a system can influence people.

Words of advice:

- Use basic facilitation techniques to focus and set a tone. Rely on ground rules and parking lots (or other means to capture topics to discuss in future).
- Maintain the right to facilitate. Build techniques for controlling the physical or virtual room—standing up to take back control during a discussion, walking in the general area of a side conversation to pull attention back to the central issue, pausing the flow to ask if everyone is ready to move on, or directly indicating the use of the right to facilitate for continuing the process. Nurture facilitation skills among several, or all, team members.
- Don't waste anyone's time. Who has a direct stake in the outcome of this meeting? If not, don't invite them. Is there an aligned purpose? Are participants engaged in collaborative exercises to help achieve this purpose? Or are they multitasking?
- Acknowledge that everyone engages in different ways. Discern which behaviors are impeding communication

and collaboration, and which are merely not your preference. Don't excuse inappropriate behavior, but welcome and have compassion for stylistic variations and preferences.

- Hold up a mirror. When the system affects team connections, it can be hard to notice. Shine a spotlight on the bigger causes and impacts. This opens the door for discussion and helps the team diminish destructive blaming responses.

Avoiding Conflict Escalation

We tend to react as if all conflict is the same. Not knowing the levels of conflict gets in the way of embracing conflict as something trying to emerge. Healthy conflict shows up as a problem to solve. A conflict masquerades as a team dilemma, incompatible goals, or a personality clash. Unfortunately, few people are taught how to collaborate well with others. So this means conflict can quickly and easily escalate to unhealthy (Figure 7.2).[2]

After a company moved to a new building, an executive held a retrospective for senior managers. While discussing the ease of access to break areas, the people manager raised a problem. The third floor had an area that connected to an outdoor roof patio. Unfortunately, the only access was via five stairs. This didn't accommodate disabled accessibility. (Conflict level: Find a solution)

During the initial design, the facilities team had this very debate but never reached consensus. As a result, the facilities manager made the final decision. This design was acceptable because the inside part of the break room was accessible. The facilities manager disagreed with the people manager about there being a problem. He stated that he didn't want to dive back into the debate with yet another group. He bluntly stated, "More than

Figure 7.2 Escalating Conflict Model

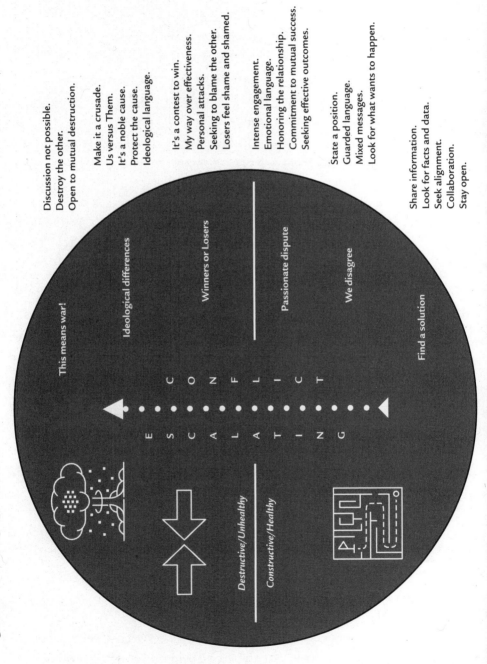

This means war!
- Discussion not possible.
- Destroy the other.
- Open to mutual destruction.

Ideological differences
- Make it a crusade.
- Us versus Them.
- It's a noble cause.
- Protect the cause.
- Ideological language.

Winners or Losers
- It's a contest to win.
- My way over effectiveness.
- Personal attacks.
- Seeking to blame the other.
- Losers feel shame and shamed.

Passionate dispute
- Intense engagement.
- Emotional language.
- Honoring the relationship.
- Commitment to mutual success.
- Seeking effective outcomes.

We disagree
- State a position.
- Guarded language.
- Mixed messages.
- Look for what wants to happen.

Find a solution
- Share information.
- Look for facts and data.
- Seek alignment.
- Collaboration.
- Stay open.

CONFLICT

ESCALATING

Destructive/Unhealthy
Constructive/Healthy

half of the break area space is available and meets requirements. This is not an issue." (Conflict level: We disagree)

The concerned people manager quickly responded, with her voice rising, "Some access is not the same thing as full access. The roof area is a space where I can see many teams wanting to gather. I'm not nitpicking here. This is important." This immediately caused the annoyed facilities manager to passionately say, "I know you care about people. But trust me, I'm doing my job. We are good. This meets the requirements for people to congregate." (Conflict level: Passionate dispute)

Before the people manager had a chance to respond, the facilities manager said, slightly under his breath, "I realize that not everyone understands the law and building codes. I know I'm right." (Conflict level: Winners or losers)

Now the irate people manager felt dismissed, and she mockingly said, "I'm not talking about the legal aspects. I'm talking about doing what is right for our teams. I probably will never go out there, but anyone in this company should have not only the right but easy access. I can't believe your team is not respecting that!" Now feeling protective of his team, the facilities manager fired back with, "You don't know the challenges my team faces! We make sure people are safe and our company is financially protected. My team is very concerned about making sure everyone is successful in this building. It's our job, and one that we are passionate about. Be glad you don't have to make the difficult decisions we face. I would love to see you do my job for even a day!" (Conflict level: Ideological differences)

The people manager slowly sat down and calmly said, "I'm done."

The facilitator announced, "Let's come back in 10 minutes when we've cooled off a bit."

In our experience, conflict can move between levels rather quickly and frequently. For **the "we disagree" conflict level**, focus the energy back toward their shared goal. This centers people back on learning for **the "find a solution" conflict level**—for example, reinforcing the value of engaging many perspectives to achieve their shared goal.

For **the "passionate dispute" conflict level**, people may experience greater discomfort due to varying styles of engagement. They may even misinterpret this conflict as unhealthy. Learning leaders allow and support passions and emotions in the workplace. They highlight and encourage building on the trust and commitment they have in the team. For example, they express compassion in times of intense learning. They thank the team for caring so much about a problem and for being courageously vulnerable with their emotions. Then they inquire how to honor their differences and each other during this discussion. This creates connections that help to de-escalate to a lower level of conflict.

For **the "winners or losers" conflict level**, collaboration skills deteriorate quickly. Participants reduce their willingness and ability to be compassionate and listen. Ego and pride take precedence in winning the conflict. Learning leaders elevate complexity and the system view. They reiterate that shame and winning are contrary to team goals. For example, demonstrate confidence in the team. Ask questions that help the team focus back on learning. What's our purpose? What's helping or hindering psychological safety right now? How well are we listening to each other right now? What are we willing to learn? These questions highlight responsibility that helps de-escalate to a lower level of conflict.

For **the "ideological differences" conflict level**, buckle up! People have taken on a rescuer role to save others. They are no longer trying to win for themselves. Now they are noble champions in their quest to protect others. Their willingness to rethink a position diminishes. Their willingness to collaborate together lessens. They feel obligated to not let others down, and trust diminishes. At this point, learning leaders help to reset and restart, possibly from scratch. For example, to courageously demonstrate taking a pause helps. Announce a break for people to walk, which sends oxygen up to the brain. This helps humans calm down to reengage at a lower level.

In the workplace, **the "this means war" conflict level** is rarely reached. Even in the moment, people are aware that certain behaviors result in termination. Plus, the previous level of conflict is so uncomfortable. Typically, someone intervenes and ends the exchange before escalating to this level.

Learning leaders want people to share commitment and responsibility for the work. The ideal conflict level is **finding a solution**. With a solid foundation of trust and commitment, resilient learning teams embrace the first three levels of conflict as healthy. But the team is composed of humans. So when conflict levels become destructive (the last three levels), learning leaders help the team de-escalate.

To be successful in de-escalation, help the team build co-intelligence on defensive mechanisms. Our brains are amazing protection systems. When facing something uncomfortable, they can unconsciously trigger a defensive response mechanism. This means that in the moment, a person may be completely unaware of their defensive reaction, thus escalating conflict levels without intent. There are many defensive mechanisms.[3] In particular, the following ones break down trust, and increase blame, in the workplace:

- Projection: Misattributing thoughts or feelings you have to someone else
- Displacement: Redirecting strong reactions toward someone who is less threatening
- Rationalization: Explaining a situation with your own set of facts for justification
- Reaction formation: Behaving in the opposite extreme from how you feel

- Intellectualization: Attempting to remove all emotion and only focus on facts

These mechanisms attempt to protect, hide, and distract from real communication of the issue. They lead back to blaming and shaming. For example, in the new building story presented earlier, both managers felt defensive. The facilities manager intellectualized with the focus on legally meeting the codes. The people manager fell into reaction formation with the calm declaration implying no interest in continuing the conversation.

Teams have to work hard to get past those initial defensive reactions during conflict. Learning leaders build awareness of the complexity of humans, because if they can communicate, then healthy conflict happens.

Words of advice:

- Provide the team a common vocabulary for discussing conflict. Shared terms remove the stigma of discussing conflict, heightening awareness and increasing the ability to candidly address the conflict.
- Normalize defensive mechanisms. Individuals can learn to improve self-awareness and manage their reactions. For example, a team may choose to have a symbolic item that an individual can hold up to show the team they are feeling defensive, indicating that they may need a minute to process before continuing.
- Agree to support the right to pause for any individual. Right to pause provides autonomy for the individual to choose to observe, to take an individual break, or to remove themselves from the conversation for now. The team respects and trusts their choice and holds no judgment. And it avoids trying to convince them to stay.

- Ensure that all relevant voices in the conflict are being heard. This means others invite and understand the points stated. This doesn't mean agreement with what is being said. Be sure to check in with each person regarding their readiness to share and whether they feel heard.
- Learn to say, "I'm sorry for . . . ," and mean it. We can cause problems even when we don't intend that outcome. Having the humility and showing the vulnerability to say sorry goes a long way to building trust. Practice these phrases: "I'm sorry that what I did caused this issue for you"; "I'm sorry that this happened. In the future, I will do [such and such] to keep it from happening again"; and "I apologize. I see my part in our misunderstanding. Can we solve the problem together?" Practicing will make it easier when the situation calls for a sincere apology.

Engaging Conflict—Feedback

Many people try to avoid conflict at all costs. Not only is this a way to guarantee conflict escalation, it also prevents and even decreases trust and resiliency in teams.

> *Tricia was once assigned as the new team leader. Her boss said, "You will love this team. There is no conflict ever." Uh-oh. Turns out there was no conflict, but it wasn't because they were effective. It was because they never spoke to each other. EVER. That's a group of individual contributors, not a team.*

Let's oversimplify conflict situations. One or more people do something different, then get verbal or nonverbal feedback. When they handle this feedback well, conflict remains healthy; it's a joint problem to solve. When they handle the feedback poorly, conflict escalates.

Yes, it is important to recognize that conflict is crucial to success. It is also important to recognize that engaging may be stressful. For some people, hearing the words, "May I give you feedback?" causes anxiety. Even if the feedback is about a trivial matter, you are on heightened alert, ready to react. Our brains focus on survival and do not distinguish between physical and social threats.[4]

A new team member cautiously tells their manager, "What I learn is valuable. But I always have such anxiety before and then leave feeling bad about myself."

Learning leaders build connections that help teams overcome the defensive mechanisms in order to keep conflict healthy. They provide them with experiences working with each other that enable them to view feedback as a gift.

People sometimes say, "Regard feedback as a gift." Really?

When someone offers you feedback, they show you who they are. *Remember the ugly, knitted, fluorescent-orange nose-warmers Great-Aunt Tilly gave you on your last birthday? You dislike this gift, but you know how long it took her to make them while caring for you in every stitch. So you keep them.*

When a giver provides feedback with care and respect, they offer a gift. When a giver provides feedback with a good intention, they offer a gift. When a giver provides feedback to build a better work connection, they offer a gift.

Receiving feedback is rarely comfortable. Just as with Great-Aunt Tilly's gift, it may not be exactly what you hoped for, yet it may have value.

Sometimes we hear about feedback that seems to be delivered as a weapon. This occurs when the giver intends to harm and shame the receiver. There is no care and respect. There is no interest in building connections. This is not feedback. This is destructive conflict.

Who delivers feedback and how they deliver it makes a difference. For example, say you hear, "Come on, I know you can do better," along with a chuckle, when someone hands back a conference speaker submission draft. From a trusted mentor, this feedback is received as a challenge to meet your full potential, and you feel grateful to have a mentor encouraging you and not settling for mediocre content. Whereas if the feedback is from a conference organizer whom you've never met, a different reaction may occur. The chuckle is interpreted as mocking. The message received feels like an insult implying the submission completely stinks. Defensive reaction mechanisms may be in full effect.

It's critical to lay groundwork for when feedback is appropriate. Otherwise, we risk negatively affecting trust and resiliency. Remember these four guidelines for feedback:

- You have firsthand, accurate, and adequate information about the circumstances surrounding the feedback.
- You've invested in making a connection. You care for and respect the recipient of the feedback. You believe this information will help them.
- You've chosen a mutually acceptable time and place, ideally delivering feedback as close to the conflict as possible.
- You are clear about the nature of the feedback and your role in giving the feedback. Is the feedback a requirement for continued employment? If so, their manager must deliver it.

Then provide the team a framework to give feedback (Figure 7.3).[5] A framework helps people stay focused on what is most important. It also helps people think about what they are going to say and how they are going to say it with care and respect.

Figure 7.3 Framework for Giving Feedback

A Framework for Giving Feedback

(1) Create an inviting opening

(2) Share intent behind the feedback

(3) Describe the specific behavior or results

(4) State the impact and continued effects

(5) Acknowledge your part

(6) Make a request

(7) Listen to the response

A Discourage and Change Feedback Example

Lou, can we connect after this morning's meeting? (Opening to negotiate setting)

This is hard, but I know the importance of collaborating together, and I want us to continue to have a great work relationship (invested intent). When we are pairing and I see you pick your teeth with your fingernail, then start typing again right afterward (specific firsthand information), I feel awkward. I become uneasy because I don't want to touch the keyboard with your saliva on it. If this continues, I won't be able to partner with you anymore (impact and role). I avoided mentioning this, which helped it become a bigger issue (own part). What I'd like is for you to wash your hands before typing, or to clean the keyboard before we switch. Or maybe we could get another keyboard so we each have one when we partner (request). Would you be willing to do any of those things? What ideas do you have? (Listen)

An Encourage and Amplify Feedback Example

Arvinder, is this a good time to talk? (Opening to negotiate setting)

   I'd like to share with you something you do that has really helped me out this week (invested intent). I was venting to Fiona that I was having a hard time completing the report. I noticed that when you overheard me, you dropped your task to come work with me until I understood how to proceed (specific firsthand information). I felt relieved that you were willing to help out with no notice and grateful for the progress on that report (impact and role). Thanks to your actions, I realize that I should have asked for help much sooner (own part). I hope you'll feel free to come offer me help anytime or ask me for help (request). [Wait for a response (listen).]

Resilient learning teams build fluency not just in giving feedback with this framework but also in receiving it. How we receive feedback also can determine the course of the conflict. Learning leaders help the team internalize these powerful receiving tips:

- Remember to breathe. It reduces stress and allows you to stay alert.
- Listen carefully. Don't interrupt or discourage the giver.
- Ask questions for clarity, not out of defensiveness.
- Acknowledge the feedback and the intent to help. Repeat the message in your own words to confirm understanding of what was said.
- The giver had time to prepare. As a recipient, take time to sort out what you heard. If needed, set a specific time for continuing the conversation.
  - Acknowledge the valid points. Agree with what's true and possible. Agreeing with what's true doesn't mean you agree to change any behaviors.

- ○ Keep what you can use. If you don't like the feedback you hear or think it doesn't fit, keep what is useful to know about yourself. As with other gifts, you can always "return feedback to the store" and disregard it. But there may be consequences to discarding feedback. For example, if not resolved, performance improvement plan feedback might lead to termination.
- If you're willing to make a change, let the giver know and describe your plan for change.
- If you're unwilling to make a change, follow three steps: (1) Explain your intent and interests. (2) Set your limits. (3) Offer to find a different, mutually satisfying alternative.
- For positive feedback, say thank you. Don't dismiss, deflect, or invalidate the feedback. Accept it and think more about it later.

Learning leaders courageously advocate for time to build co-intelligence with this framework, from both the giver and the receiver perspectives. Everyone embraces the complexity of human reactions to feedback. Compassion and listening help conflict remain healthy. Over time, confidence builds in the team's ability to give, receive, and seek feedback. All contribute to keeping conflicts healthy. These kinds of conversations challenge us to be our best selves. Engaging feedback becomes a little easier because we see the results in mutual growth. That's motivating. And we become a stronger, more resilient team.

Words of advice:

- Practice small feedback loops. Be brief. The most effective feedback is short, simple, and to the point. Give specific, recent examples for one focused topic.

- Highlight exact behavior, not general impressions. Restrict feedback to things—*you saw, you heard, you read, you feel, you want.*
- Avoid inflammatory language, labels, and exaggerations like *always* or *never*. Avoid judgment words that set up an adversarial tone like *good, worst,* or *should. Should* is one of Diana's pet peeves: "Don't should on me!" It can come across as finger-wagging or manipulative. Try replacing *should* with *could* for better results.
- Speak for yourself and encourage others to speak for themselves. Receiving feedback through a third person often breaks trust. Offer opportunities to practice feedback situations to build team communication skills. Offer to role-play with a colleague who is anxious about specific feedback.
- Avoid mixing messages during feedback. The "feedback sandwich" approach of "encourage, discourage, encourage" is ineffective. This approach may make the feedback easier for the giver, but the results are poor. Typically, the recipient is thinking, "Whatever. I'm waiting for the shoe to drop. Yep, there is the gut punch. I don't want a pity compliment." Givers can become concerned that recipients will "get complacent" with encouragement. For example, "The team went above and beyond to get this report finished on time. But I know you can do even better next time. Our customers are so excited." This approach completely misses the mark on how to challenge a team. We have never seen a team receive encouraging feedback and respond by ceasing to work. Some of the best growth is building on something you are already succeeding at.

Figure 7.4 Retrospectives for Resilience

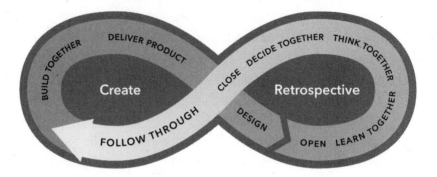

Retrospectives for Resilience
Inspect and Adapt Systems and Teamwork

BUILD TOGETHER · DELIVER PRODUCT · **Create** · FOLLOW THROUGH · CLOSE · DECIDE TOGETHER · THINK TOGETHER · **Retrospective** · DESIGN · OPEN · LEARN TOGETHER

Example Design

Leaders build resilient learning teams by highlighting underlying challenges, especially conflict—not once but continuously along the way. They invite the team to use a retrospective to explore specific topics. As a leader, you don't get to decide what the team's outcome action items are. Yet you can choose to focus on the area where you've observed the team is struggling. The retrospective example given here showcases how leaders promote healthy conflict guided by the Retrospectives for Resilience (Figure 7.4). Note that this is not the only retrospective design for this specific topic. This example showcases reinforcing the essential motivators and resilience factors.

Scenario

Refer back to the story earlier in this chapter about the new team of administrators who chose to perform an experiment of using the new approach with a few customers, then review the approach at the next retrospective. This is the design for that second retrospective.

Retrospective Logistics

- **Facilitator intent:** Logistics influence the *setting* to ensure it supports the team's learning
- **Setting:** Mixed, some people online and some people in person
- **Number of participants:** Invited six in person and three online
- **Duration:** 90 minutes (1:30–3:00 p.m.)
- **Day:** Thursday
- **Food:** NA
- **Location:** On-site with video conference capabilities
- **Setup:** Videoconference tool and remote collaboration tool. One U-shaped table set up with each person having their own computer in front of them. Share a single audio source for the room. Accessory table for supplies, including flip charts, markers, sticky notes, and so on. Alternatively, remove the shared room and have everyone be online.

Retrospective Design

The retrospective design provides a process outline for the facilitator to accomplish the goal.

Set the Stage (10 Minutes)

- **Facilitator intent:** To help everyone participate at the start of the retrospective and to build shared experience and trust (*collaborative connection*). To align on the topic or outcome. To encourage learning, collaboration, and creativity (*alive*). To model and set the tone for blame-free engagement and increase safety. To provide activities that keep the team's *purpose obvious* by focusing on real work (*fluency*) aspects right from the beginning. To acknowledge that the focus on a topic that has generated previous conflicts requires compassion and listening (*embracing conflict*).

- **Overall retrospective agenda**
- **Topic:** Interviewing approach pilot experiment—what's next?
- **Outcome:** Keep as is or define one to two revisions to the interviewing approach experiment.
- **Activity:** Motivation, trust, and safety exercise from Chapter 6. Note: As this team has done this exercise several times, there is no need to explain it.

Gather Data (20 Minutes)

- **Facilitator intent:** To create safety for exploring this topic with choice on individual contributions (*autonomy*). To increase visibility, internalization, and normalization of the data being shared (*fluency*). Pulling each team member's perspective on the work so far makes the whole team experience more *obvious* to everyone and builds the momentum of *co-intelligence*. Note that data about conflict will include both objective and subjective aspects (*embracing conflict*).
- **Data**: Present the information: How many people were interviewed? How long did the interviews last? How many people provided feedback after the interview?
- **Activity:** For the interviewing approach experiment, add sticky notes to the sailboat graphic on the online whiteboard.[6] What helped sail? What held back (anchored)? Add notes about subjective data. To minimize unhealthy conflict, reinforce that all experiences are valuable in helping the team make a collaborative decision.

Generate Insights (35 Minutes)

- **Facilitator intent:** To generate several new ideas for the interviewing approach experiment tied to the challenges experienced. To achieve iterative improvement to the process. To encourage all voices and respectful examination of ideas, impacts, implications, and challenges (*collaborative connection*). To explore the feasibility of new insights and experiments emerging (*co-intelligence*). Staying focused with targeted questions helps momentum (*obvious*). Gathering insights relies on collaborative learning, analysis, internalizing, and identifying options (*fluency* and *co-intelligence*). Try out low-stakes techniques for managing conflict as a technique for increasing *fluency* with conflicts during real work (*embracing conflict*).

- **Activity or tool:** Put "What if?" in the center of a mindmap, which is a visual tool for identifying and organizing concepts.[7] Encourage adding and describing each new revision idea based on information from the sailboat activity. Discuss the main reason for each revision. Encourage building off each other's ideas and exploring what is possible rather than focusing on roadblocks. Continue to revise the mindmap during the discussion with new, changed, or removed ideas or concerns.

Decide What to Do (15 Minutes)

- **Facilitator intent:** Ideally to converge on the action items that have the most energy and interest (*alive*). To bring the team together to decide the action items to improve the work (*fluency*) that everyone can support (*purpose*) (*autonomy*), with equal voices and volunteering encouraging *collaborative connection.*

- **Activity or tool:** Use the poll to identify the proposed revisions that generate the most impact with energy from team members. Post the mindmap revisions remaining and keep as-is options, then have a ranked-choice vote. Each team member chooses their first, second, and third favorite and votes accordingly. Then request two volunteers to lead the experiment for the actions with the most energy voted.

Close the Retrospective (5 Minutes)

- **Facilitator intent:** To intentionally remind everyone of the goal and the mindsets required for success, while keeping the activity short (*alive*). To reinforce effective work relationships (*collaborative connection*), with the goal of fostering a shared team purpose.
- **Activity or tool:** Conduct a survey of team evolution, using Figure 2.3 as a guide. Ask the team, "Our engagement today most reflected what stage?"
  Note: This retrospective event was scheduled for 90 minutes. The design accounts for 85 minutes. The additional 5 minutes is buffer time for unexpected adjustments to the design. For example, the group may need more time for a discussion than was planned.

Leadership through learning requires becoming comfortable with individual and team conflicts. Learning to embrace conflict holds more value than attempting to deal with the consequences of avoiding conflict. Healthy conflict helps grow and enable resilient learning teams. Retrospectives offer one tangible way to promote healthy conflict and address unhealthy conflicts. In this design, the *flow* of activities promoted conflict to remain healthy by starting with *compassion* and *courage* to bring awareness of the motivation, trust, and safety in the moment. By encouraging team members to build on each other's ideas, thus *confidently* minimizing unhealthy conflict. By exploring what is possible rather than focusing on roadblocks. By providing people with opportunities to demonstrate *complexity* in their decisions. By inviting team members to start and inviting volunteers to move forward. By ending with a reminder of the team's desired evolution. All these together grow stronger, more resilient learning teams.

With each retrospective that reinforces healthy conflict, learning leaders help the team build resiliency.

But What If . . . ?

- *Due to a conflict, people refuse to work together?*
  Regardless of its level, if a conflict is left unresolved, trust will continue to degrade. It will get to the point that active distrust is present. Yet repairing the connection may be possible. Unpack the source of the conflict. If the conflict has a long duration or is a complex topic, be patient and find connections to rebuild trust. Sometimes, sadly, restoring trust is impossible without a complete change in setting. For more on identifying the sources of conflict, see Esther Derby's blog post "5 Sources of Team Conflict."[8]
- *There is always one specific person involved in every conflict, and that person is a problem?*
  We prefer to give our team members the benefit of the doubt. They may have learned dysfunctional team behavior from other people or environments. Learning leaders model and teach the behaviors expected in resilient learning teams. If that doesn't help with the dysfunctional behaviors, give feedback. Listen for other factors that are likely contributing to the situation.

That said, people can and do bring toxic behavior to the workplace. Someone may continue to behave badly even after receiving feedback more than once. If you find yourself saying, "That's just Mike," recognize the justification. Tolerating bad behavior damages others. Now it's an HR issue. The person's behavior affects the performance of the whole team. They are no longer a good fit. Escalate the problem and expect resolution.

- *No matter what we try, conflict always seems to escalate to destructive levels?*
  Call it out. Offer a reset. Chances are you skipped or spent too little effort on trust and commitment. There may not be sufficient connections or meaningful purpose enabling compassion and collaboration. Offer learning opportunities to develop conflict skills.

- *Conflicts derail the shorter retrospectives?*
  A series of short, focused retrospectives can be extremely effective. With strong facilitation and designs, the chances diminish for a conflict to derail an entire retrospective. But sometimes, conflict seems to be coming from everywhere. Adjust the retrospective design toward reinforcing positive energy in the team. Occasionally, focus solely on building on what the team is doing well. People want to feel capable and good about themselves and their work. This gives them the opportunity to view and connect with the bigger picture beyond their conflicts.

Reflections for Your Learning

Begin embracing the conflict resilience factor today. Learning leaders focus intensely on resilient learning for the organization, teams, and themselves.

How do behavior challenges create conflicts in your
   organization?

How have conflicts escalated? How might you have
   avoided those escalations?

How customary is giving, receiving, and seeking feedback
   in your organization?

Who is one person with whom you could practice the
   feedback framework?

How does the level of trust and commitment influence
   conflict?

How could you adapt the example to fit your organization? What similarities and differences would you
   expose?

How do the Learning Leaders 4Cs (compassion, complexity, confidence, and courage) mitigate conflict?

CHAPTER 8

The Inclusive Collaboration Resilience Factor

R ead this. Yes, READ THIS. This chapter is for you. If you decide to skip a chapter, pick a different one. As we wrote a book
about continuous learning, we also learned ourselves. If we could
go back in time as leaders, we would invest more in workplace inclusion. Since time travel is not an option, we are doing it now.

This chapter about inclusion factors was challenging for us to
write. Inclusion is a much broader effort than either of us realized. We are not inclusion experts. As such, we were lucky to collaborate and learn with Gilmara Vila Nova-Mitchell, a diversity,
equity, and inclusion (DEI) consultant.

As leaders, we thought we were being inclusive. Neither one of
us thought we were actively discriminating against or excluding
people. Our leadership focus has always been to create spaces
where people can excel. We acknowledge that we had success in
some cases and missed the mark in others. These experiences
gave us some insight into the challenges of workplace inclusion.
Of course, we've each had our own path.

Diana's early journey coincided with the civil rights and feminist movements of the 1970s and early 1980s. Her learning continued through the backlash of the next decades.

*As I entered the work world in the mid-1980s, I discovered that
many women had stepped away from the "sisterhood" of feminism.*

It seemed especially like a touchy subject when applied in work-places. My own experiences of discrimination as a woman at work showed me that things hadn't changed much. I could identify the obvious behavior norms that discounted people. In my work, I eagerly accepted assignments with aspects of diversity and equity. For example, I took on the opportunity to facilitate company special interest groups. I learned more about diversity issues than the special interest group members learned about facilitating. Yet "inclusion" as a topic wasn't on our agendas.

I was glad that other consultants engaged in diversity training and consulting practices. I focused on talent development and improving work processes. At the time, I didn't perceive the overlap of their concerns with mine. So I stayed in my own lane.

In the late 1990s, my business partner, a few female colleagues, and I started a nonprofit. We wanted to support learning and education for women in leadership roles. We wanted to understand and share their paths to success. At the time, our focus was on increasing the number of women in workplace leadership. We thought the path led through preparing women to be better leaders. We promoted ideas about ways women could show they "fit in" and prove their competence. Our focus was on women, not on the changes that organizations needed to create more inclusive environ-ments. My nonprofit cofounders continued to look for ways to support women at work. Life took me in another direction—agile!

Along the way, I found my own place as a leader in our agile software development evolution. Yet I still encountered gender discrimination. I used those experiences to fuel my intense focus on equity where I had immediate influence. My work shifted to mak-ing workplaces healthier in a broad way. I knew healthy, humane workplaces would lead to greater success for clients. Dealing with daily workplace inclusion felt like tilting at windmills. So I decided to keep my own workplace in a small business. Pragmatically, I remained in an external consulting and coaching role where I chose my work environments. This way I could work with people who respected each other and enjoyed working together. Looking back, I see that I created a comfortable, productive bubble and assumed I could stay in it.

My thinking received a jolt from the societal bias events of 2015–2021. It renewed my awareness of discrimination against underrepresented people in tech, including women. While I had made some difference, it no longer felt like enough. I needed to expand my view beyond my lane. Getting in the door was still a challenge for many people. And we needed much more emphasis on what happens once they or we take a seat. It isn't enough to work toward workforce diversity. We need to be vocal about inclusive work environments as well.

When Tricia left her small hometown in the 1990s, her learning about inequities really began. College was a different environment with a vast diversity of experiences. Little did she understand then, her learning would be lifelong.

I was explicitly taught that certain topics were not appropriate for the workplace. I learned to not discuss differences among colleagues. Generally, I followed this guidance. Except I did have discussions in my individual connections with people. I would privately ask questions that seemed professionally off-limits. I'm grateful for those countless conversations. I learned about challenges others faced that had been invisible to me. For example, a colleague shared his frustrations about the visa application process. His application had been repeatedly lost. With each application restart, he felt more trapped and powerless. I had no idea he was struggling or that this even happens!

Each private conversation with colleagues increased my awareness and compassion for other people's experiences with inclusion. Yet, publicly, I still adhered to the "We don't discuss that at work" norm. I even declined a request that was based on the tenets of the person's religion. Today, I'm ashamed to admit that decision, that I had convinced myself that the responsibility to adapt was theirs. Oh, how I would handle this request differently now.

For about the first 20 years of my career, I compartmentalized. I had different rules personally and professionally. Fast-forward to around 2016. At that time a perfect storm of events helped me realize that I needed to learn and grow. I intensified my focus on creating space and amplifying underrepresented people. I challenged myself to engage in difficult conversations regardless of the setting. Then one moment unlocked a significant learning experience that motivates me to be better.

At a conference, I was walking down the hall. As I was about to turn the corner, I heard my name. Person X was asking a colleague of mine, "Was Tricia the token female?" My colleague's response was incredibly complimentary, yet it felt inadequate. Now let me be 100 percent transparent. I have responded to similar questions about others with compliments too. Yet I found myself being upset that my colleague didn't challenge the inappropriateness of the question. As a woman in a male-dominated industry, after all these years and accomplishments, I am tired, exhausted from continually proving myself in ways that go above and beyond what is expected of my male colleagues. While this question was not new, my disappointment in my colleague was. Why didn't my colleague call out this inappropriate question to create inclusion for me and others?

That colleague and I still have a wonderful relationship today. I share this story because it was the moment I realized the series of errors I had made. I assumed that opening doors for diversity automatically led to inclusion. Yet here I was, standing in a hallway, not feeling valued or included. Good intentions, abilities, accomplishments, compliments, and respected connections didn't prevent trust from breaking a little that day.

This moment changed me as a leader and as a person. No more compartmentalizing. No more avoiding. If I want to create spaces where people can excel, intentional inclusion matters. Thank you to every single person who has helped me learn along this continuing journey. I can't change the past, and I won't always get it right. But I promise to keep trying to foster inclusive collaboration in the workplace.

Our stories are different and yet similar. And we recognize our privilege. We understand that we each have a small collection of experiences within a wide set of inclusion challenges. All around us, people have stories about the failure of inclusion in the workplace. The question is, "Are we listening?"

Diversity, Equity, and Inclusion

Many organizations have begun their journey to improve DEI.[1] Yet there remains confusion on exactly what this means and how it applies to teams.

Diversity: Celebrating the presence of differences. Differences may include race, gender, religion, sexual orientation, ethnicity, nationality, socioeconomic status, language, (dis)ability, age, religious commitment, and political perspective.

Equity: Promoting justice, impartiality, and fairness, including in institutional or systemic procedures, processes, and distribution of resources.

Inclusion: Ensure that all team members feel welcomed and feel that they belong. They participate fully and authentically in the decision-making processes and opportunities within an organization.

Figure 8.1 Equality, Equity, and Inclusion

The left-hand image in Figure 8.1 represents **equality**. Equality is when everyone gets the exact same thing. This may or may not create the ability for everyone to engage or contribute.

The middle image represents **equity**. Equity is when everyone gets what they need to be able to engage. A focus on equity ensures that underrepresented individuals have access to opportunities, resources, and practices in the workplace. People with privilege may focus on what they didn't get and what others are getting, then perceive that the system is unfair.

The right-hand image represents **inclusion**. Inclusion is when everyone's needs are met (equity) and, in addition, they can engage fully and authentically. Inclusion means everyone belongs. I'm welcomed. I'm meant to be here. I'm accepted and embraced. My perspective is valuable and wanted.

When organizations focus on increasing diversity, they gain potential. They build the ability to achieve the benefits of collaboration. Collaboration is people learning and building together. The best collaboration comes from a wealth of knowledge, experiences, and perspectives. As organizations increase equity, they add policies that amplify the benefits of diversity. Equity may appear to make things more fair, but it only really helps address an immediate need.

Giving attention to diversity and equity opens doors and gives people a seat at the table. Yet it doesn't guarantee that people can contribute at the table. Organizations that focus on increasing inclusion achieve the benefits from diversity and equity.

When organizations foster a setting of inclusive collaboration, it's good for business. People are able to build the right products for the diverse landscape of this world. It makes a place for more creative and innovative people who build the products right. According to Deloitte's article on diversity and inclusion, "A growing body of research indicates that diverse and inclusive teams outperform their peers. Companies with inclusive talent practices in hiring, promotion, development, leadership, and team management generate up to 30 percent higher revenue per employee and greater profitability than their competitors."[2]

To achieve team resiliency, learning leaders must resolutely concentrate on inclusive collaboration. This chapter only scratches the surface of DEI. We focus on these foundational DEI elements as related to inclusive collaboration in the workplace.

Let's revisit Soniya's team (from Part Two) and their struggles with going remote. Here's an example of interactions that contributed to breaking their high-performing team.

One team member jokingly commented that Dillon's remote computer setup was outdated and archaic. The joking team member tried to be helpful by providing a link on Amazon for updated technology. As the weeks went by, Dillon's setup remained the same. The jokes increased. When the jokes started, Dillon tried laughing it off. However, as they became more hurtful, he kept looking to the leader, Soniya, to interject, but she remained silent.

Dillon didn't want to share that he had helped a family member by paying for her divorce and relocation. Because of this and other burdens, he was tight on finances. Soniya had offered that each person could buy necessary equipment and expense it to the company. But this was not a helpful solution for Dillon because he didn't have the funds to spare upfront. He didn't want to admit this in front of everyone, so he began avoiding remote interactions.

As a learning leader, be courageously willing to have these difficult conversations. Soniya's silence sent mixed messages that inhibited inclusive collaboration. Silence may imply a position, just maybe not the one you intended. Soniya's silence was interpreted as permission for other team members to shame Dillon if they made it sound like a joke.

Many people think they require trust before they can create inclusion. Not so. Trust results from inclusion. Leaders may assume they've addressed inclusion because they don't hear complaints. But in this example, Dillon didn't feel safe to share. This exclusion had an impact on later actions, such as when Dillon avoided remote interactions. Imagine what actions might happen after these situations:

- Gossip and rumors imply that a promotion was based on behaviors unrelated to work.
- Assumptions are made in assigning who will do the low-status or unpaid work.
- There is a generalized expectation of an individual that denies their abilities.

Learning leaders compassionately ask the following questions early and often:

- Is everyone's voice heard and their point of view included?
- Does everyone experience welcoming accommodations?
- Does everyone belong and feel a part of something bigger?

- Is everyone respectful of others?
- Does everyone feel their career can progress?

Intersectionality

Conceptualized and named by Kimberlé Williams Crenshaw, intersectionality is an analytical framework.[3] It helps people to understand how aspects of a person's social and political identities combine. The combinations create different modes of discrimination and privilege. Examples of these factors include gender, caste, sex, race, class, sexuality, religion, disability, and physical appearance (Figure 8.2).

Each factor intersects and overlaps to create identities. These may be both empowering and oppressing. The following are some examples:

- A Christian female can experience privilege in a US workplace holiday schedule. The schedule aligns with

Figure 8.2 Intersectionality Example

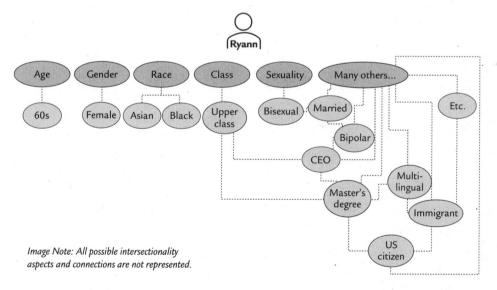

Image Note: All possible intersectionality aspects and connections are not represented.

her personal needs. Yet she may experience oppression from having no female senior leadership role models.

- A Black female is experiencing wage discrimination at a business. The discrimination may not be due solely to her race, as the business does not wage discriminate against Black men. The discrimination may not be due solely to her gender, as the business does not wage discriminate against women. Yet, as an individual with a combination identity, she experiences something different.

When a work colleague arrives, they bring their competencies. They also bring experiences and outlooks from their unique intersectionalities. As you become more aware of others' intersectionalities, embrace those differences. They help unlock more insights into customer needs with a broader perspective on issues. They increase co-intelligence for problem solving. They elevate the capacity to innovate. They help the team build resiliency to differences, to the unknown, to complexity, and to making space for others. This is inclusive collaboration.

Learning leaders must invite and openly support these unique intersectional experiences. Honor the differences of individuals' identity factors, their backgrounds, and their personal experiences. At the same time, respect people's willingness to share or remain private about their intersectionality. No one individual can speak on behalf of everyone.

Words of advice:

- Start with your own stories. Learning leaders are more influential when they role-model rather than simply telling others. Demonstrating vulnerability while valuing differences helps build trust.

- Openly and humbly acknowledge your mistakes when it comes to including others. Approach your interactions with a growth mindset. The more curious we become, the less judgmental we are.
- Surround yourself with people who are different from you. Listen to them and broaden your perspective.
- Celebrate collaboration successes that have achieved powerful outcomes because of diverse inclusion. Notice and comment on the small successes, as well as the big, splashy ones.
- Assess the diverse perspectives necessary for high-value delivery. Be intentional about team representation. You may never have (or need) 100 percent representation of all intersectionality factors.
- Intentionally create space for people to get to know each other personally. With permission, incorporate exercises that respectfully explore intersectionality with the team members. Boost awareness of what every team member brings to the joint effort. Highlight how their differences contribute value to the whole team's work. Again, people can share as much of their stories as they feel comfortable sharing.
- Be mindful of the language you use in everyday interactions. If you want to be inclusive, your words need to reflect that intention.

Workplace Microaggressions

In 1974 Chester Pierce coined the term *microaggression* to refer to a statement, action, or incident regarded as an instance of indirect, subtle, or unintentional discrimination against members of a marginalized group.[4] Microaggressions can occur in any intersectionality segment.

Derald Wing Sue, author of *Race Talk*, created this definition of *microaggression*: "Brief and commonplace daily verbal, behavioral, or environmental indignities, whether intentional or unintentional, that communicate hostile, derogatory, or negative racial slights and insults toward people of color."[5]

Microaggressions are not generally intended to be hurtful. But intent is not as important as impact. The sheer number of intersectionalities means people are more likely both to deliver and to receive microaggressions. The workplace is no exception. People whose intersectional background lands in dominant groups deliver significantly more. They also receive significantly fewer. This imbalance results from bias. Within each intersectionality, there is the potential for conscious (known and intentional) and unconscious bias.

All humans have unconscious bias. It is a natural response to processing massive amounts of information. Our brains put things in categories to quickly make sense of something. Unfortunately, biases affect how we form connections. Unconscious biases work under the surface without people realizing. They ultimately lead people to include or exclude others by group rather than by getting to know individuals. The following are some example scenarios of unconscious bias's impact in the workplace:

Unconscious bias: Also known as implicit bias, *unconscious bias* refers to the attitudes, perceptions, and stereotypes that influence our understanding, actions, and behavior when interacting with various intersectionality factors.[6] These preferences, which can be for or against identities, are developed through an exposure to stereotypes and misinformation. They are informed by our upbringing and life experiences. Residing deep in the subconscious, these biases are different from conscious biases that individuals may choose to conceal or justify.

- delivering positive hiring or performance reviews for people with similar characteristics, or negatively appraising those who differ from us
- believing that a person is less capable at performing a job based on education (degree level, prestige, etc.)
- assuming and expecting a specific visual of professionalism (attire, style, personality, etc.)

Conversely, the following are some examples of conscious bias's impact in the workplace:

- applying previous experiences to a new individual based on a generalization
- not giving a promotion to a pregnant female
- expecting individuals with dietary needs to deal with that themselves

Biases do not always remain hidden. They tend to surface via microaggressions.

At the end of his first day, Trevor was extremely tired but felt like it had gone well. As he was heading for the front door, one of his new colleagues, Mike, caught up to him. Mike gave Trevor a pat on the shoulder and said, "I was worried you would play the race card, but I really enjoyed working with you today."

In this scenario, Mike is the perpetrator, and Trevor is the recipient. There is good intent behind what the perpetrator is attempting to share, so the harm may be unintentional. For example, Mike might be trying to share how awesome working with Trevor was today. Or he might be trying to be vulnerable in saying he was nervous to work with a person of color. Despite these possible intentions, Trevor experienced a harmful impact.

He heard and felt underlying negative messages. They included the following: "People of color are difficult to work with"; "People of color only get things because of quotas or race cards"; and "People of color should feel ashamed." Recipients hear and take in messages that are influenced by previous similar microaggression experiences.

So we have Mike, who thinks he's doing a good thing, and we have Trevor, who is experiencing a bad thing. What happens next? There are two possible options: option A is that Trevor awkwardly smiles and leaves; option B is that Trevor responds to the microaggression.

At that moment, Trevor is considering several things. Will Mike be defensive and only focus on explaining his intent? Will Mike want to center the conversation on making himself feel better? Will Mike accuse him of being overly sensitive? Does Mike hold any influence over his employment?

For too long, many people chose option A to avoid the conflict. This option results in the impact of the microaggression accumulating with the trauma of previous similar statements for Trevor. Also, when microaggressions occur and continue to occur, the conflict is already destructive and trust breaks. This means that as Trevor continues to work, he may keep Mike at a distance. Trevor may remain civil, professional, and cooperative but not feel able to collaborate. As Trevor had to suppress a negative impact, he may not feel a sense of belonging in the team.

If Trevor selects option B, the interaction can go well or poorly. If it goes poorly, it could follow this typical disappointing pattern:

Recipient highlights impact
Perpetrator highlights intent
Recipient reinforces impact

Perpetrator diminishes impact because of intent and
"trivial" example
No resolution occurs

Any one microaggression example can seem trivial. Yet every microaggression adds to the total accumulated harm. The messages of bias and discrimination become bigger and louder with each microaggression. As a result, individuals who experience microaggressions regularly more commonly exhibit depression and anxiety.

Ideally, Trevor selects option B and the interaction goes well with this pattern of interaction:

Recipient highlights the microaggression using the Intent
and Impact Framework (Figure 8.3)[7]
Perpetrator reassures intent
Recipient acknowledges intent and reinforces impact
Perpetrator acknowledges impact and appreciates learning an alternative
Resolution occurs or a way to proceed is agreed on

Figure 8.3 Intent and Impact Framework

SEPARATE INTENT FROM IMPACT

I know you didn't (*realize/intend*) this,
but when you (*specific comment/behavior*),
it was (*specific* **impact**).

Optional: This is because (*specific
education/experience/background*).

Instead, you could
(*different **alternative/option** that aligns with intent*).

If you are the perpetrator, receiving feedback for a microaggression offers an opportunity. Regard it as a chance to learn something new about people and collaboration. Yes, intent matters. In fact, if you have ill intent, you are exhibiting aggression, not a microaggression. The gap between our intentions and our impacts comes from our biases. Remember, impact matters more. Learning leaders intentionally build confidence in their team's ability to foster inclusive collaboration.

Words of advice:

- Become aware of conscious biases. Explore possible unconscious biases. Take bias assessments and openly discuss intersectionality and inclusion effects.
- Practice responding to a microaggression. For the recipient, this means practicing how to respond. And for the perpetrator, it means practicing how to receive the feedback.
- Bring in DEI expertise. Consider training for teams. Consider guidance for structures, policies, and interactions.
- Provide real support to people who receive a microaggression. Dolly Chugh, *In the Person You Mean to Be*, notes how we can better support people after they receive a microaggression: "First, it is okay to be tongue-tied. . . . Second, it is not about you. . . . Third, let go of your need for affirmation. . . . Fourth, do not dodge."[8] Be compassionate and nonjudgmental. Listen with compassion. Then listen some more. When things are emotionally charged, acknowledge the information shared. Be willing to make an earnest effort not to judge or discount the person's feelings, even if you don't

necessarily understand them or feel comfortable with them. Then ask, "How would you like support?"

- Create a psychologically safe setting to engage. Typically, these interactions tend to go better in person, with a limited number of individuals involved.
- Pay close attention to your tone and body language. The more stressed someone feels, the less they can process word choices. How you speak becomes more important than what you say. When speaking to somebody you respect, your tone and body language reflect that. You become relaxed, receptive, and nonthreatening, showing a special degree of patience and attention. Your tone and body language help the individual embrace the conversation, thus taking it to heart.
- Allow silence for reflection and the processing of ideas. Too often, we share something difficult and expect an immediate response. Our brain takes at least 6–10 seconds to produce thoughtful reflection. Allowing space for silence is important, even if it may feel uncomfortable.

"Mount Stupid"

As resilient learning teams learn how to better handle the inevitable workplace microaggressions, shame may present additional challenges. In *Think Again*, Adam Grant notes that as people learn, they can get stuck on "Mount Stupid" (Figure 8.4).[9]

An issue develops in the team. There is an urgency and willingness to learn. We build some co-intelligence. Suddenly, the team declares expertise and stops learning. This point is being on top of Mount Stupid. People at this point may project overconfidence in what they know and can do (the Dunning-Kruger effect).[10] Conversely, people who never make it to Mount Stupid may show underconfidence in their competence (imposter syndrome).[11]

Figure 8.4 Mount Stupid Graph

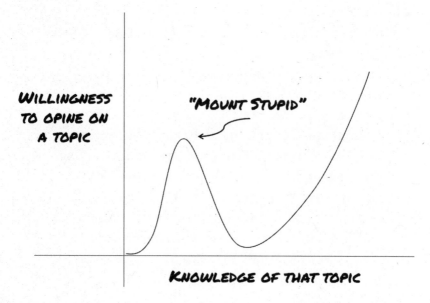

Both are protection mechanisms for dealing with blame and shame. Both exhaust people and lead to burnout.

Resilient learning teams learn how to come down from the mountain to move forward. They find the balance between knowledge and a willingness to continuously learn. They don't let protection mechanisms hold them back. Grant shares a term for a better balance focused on continuous learning: *confident humility*. Confident humility enables us to move past any fears of blame and shame to build co-intelligence.

The book *Race Talk* by Derald Wing Sue includes the developmental phases of white racial identity.[12] These stages were defined by Janet Helms and then refined by Derald Wing Sue and David Sue. They focus specifically on the intersectionality of race. We have expanded the phases to be applicable for any intersectionality factor.

- **Naïveté:** Having naive curiosity about differences. We have only innocent, open, and spontaneous questions regarding racial, gender, ability, age, and other differences. As children, we form our outlook based on responses to our questions. (*Child:* Look, Mommy, that lady has a chair with wheels! *Mommy:* Hush dear, don't point, don't notice her. *Child internalizes:* I can't ask Mommy about people like that. Disabilities are not discussed.) In general, people exit this phase by age five.
- **Conformity:** Having minimal to no awareness of the challenges that underrepresented individuals experience (e.g., the story in Chapter 7 about the conflict that arose when a company moved to a new building whose rooftop patio was only accessible via stairs). As a result, we hold a strong belief that everyone is created and treated equally. Our behavior reflects the dominant beliefs about and norms toward different experiences. Thus, our bias causes us to express microaggressions and privilege. (Overheard on Twitter: "I had to stop following [name] because they started being political talking about civil rights. That's got no place at work!") This phase can last a lifetime if we deny information.
- **Dissonance:** Gaining awareness of inconsistencies with challenges but trying to force them to make sense. We feel guilt, shame, anger, and even depression upon learning inconsistencies. We may rely on even more rationalizations to avoid our psychological discomfort—for instance, an older relative who claims to support LGBTQ+ but opposes their child being LGBTQ+ because "society won't accept it." When the discomfort becomes too great, we want and need to resolve the dissonance. Unfortunately, this often means regressing

to conformity. The challenge is to continue working through the disparity by encouraging open conversations and challenging current bias norms.

- **Resistance and immersion:** Questioning and challenging to gain insight into biases and discrimination. As we realize our past errors, missed opportunities, and current ignorance, we seek quick solutions to resolve the discomfort. We may take deep dives into material to learn more. Although there is a willingness to immerse in learning, we focus our energy more outward on changes for others rather than inward on our own outlooks and behaviors. In the quest for fast action, we may turn to reactionary, unhelpful responses, such as declaring, "All men are misogynistic; only women should be leaders." The challenge is to not let the fear of having an impact prevent deeper internal reflection.

- **Introspection:** Acknowledging personal and systematic bias, as well as focusing on altering bias through education and experience. We focus our energy appropriately inward on foundational work that enables change. In this phase, we become listeners willing to engage in tough conversations. We begin to acknowledge our past harms without centering the conversation on our growth. For example, we don't approach a former colleague for reassurance that they didn't experience harm from us two years ago. This action would be centering on our needs, not our colleague's needs. The challenge is to move beyond personal analysis into real action.

- **Integrative awareness:** Proactively challenging personal bias. We find deep value in diversity, equity, and especially inclusion. We gain greater comfort from seeking out and engaging in conversations. We take caution in choosing ways to respond to the "You make everything about . . ." reactions. We begin to learn how to use our privilege to help others effectively. This work may feel obvious to us now, but there was a journey to get to this phase. The challenge is to not get exhausted and impatient. We need to secure support to refuel. Remember the in-flight rule: when in a crisis, secure your own oxygen mask before helping others.

- **Commitment to inclusion:** Exhibiting consequential change in behavior and increased commitment to inclusion. It takes constant courage from us to correct injustice (as Senator John Lewis said, "Never, ever be afraid to make some noise and get in good trouble, necessary trouble").[13] We become increasingly immune to social pressures for conformity and avoidance of topics. We stand up for actions to include others, whatever their differences. We must continue to ensure our self-care while doing this important work.

Inclusivity is complex. With learning and experiences, people progress or regress. People may be in a later phase on one intersectionality and an earlier phase on a different one. You are not guaranteed to move through all these phases. Chugh, in *The Person You Mean to Be*, notes, "In these early stages . . . , what happens next is critical. The natural reflex is to reduce the pain and self-threat. Some individuals do this by doubling down. They might even blame the victims. Alternatively, people can stick with willful awareness and move to the next stage. They move closer to being the person they mean to be."[14]

Learning leaders help the team use these phase descriptions only for self-assessment. Do not label anyone else as being in a phase—for example, "Oh, you're just still in resistance and immersion. Get with it!" We can't know what's going on inside others.

Even if your intent is to help them by providing this information, it still feels like blame. Also, remember that each team member is free to volunteer (or not) to share their self-assessed phase.

Use the phase descriptions to reflect, increase learning, and constantly practice inclusive collaboration. Show each other compassion and patience while confronting biases. As the team's inclusion evolves, their resiliency grows.

Words of advice:

- Bias is a natural function of the brain. It is as natural as breathing. To conserve energy, our brain can produce inaccurate thoughts about groups of people. It enables you to form an opinion quickly without having to dig up the facts. This serves the function of keeping you safe in risky situations. Our work consists in reducing and mitigating the impact of our biases as we collaborate with others. The more aware you become of your biases, the more equipped you are to act appropriately and be inclusive.

- When we slip up, we have a tendency to be very hard on ourselves. We give others more compassion and understanding than we give ourselves. When you notice that you're heading into shaming, ask yourself, "What would you say to someone else?" Try having a conversation with yourself in the mirror as if you're speaking with a peer or a team member.

- Create support groups. Learning about inclusion is difficult work, and it is ongoing. Avoidance is no longer an option in the workplace. Watch for times when people need to regain energy. Find support by interacting with peers who are also engaged in building inclusive collaborations.

• Acknowledge your limitations and ask for help. Inclusion work can be triggering and traumatic. You are not a qualified therapist (unless you are!). You are not an expert in everything. Do not stay on top of Mount Stupid. There is no shame in asking for help.

Example Design

Leaders encourage their teams to become resilient learning teams by highlighting underlying challenges, not once but continuously along the way. They invite the team to use a retrospective to explore specific topics. As a leader, you don't get to decide what the team's outcome action items are. Yet you can choose to focus on the topic area where you've observed that the team is struggling. The retrospective example given here showcases how teams focus on building inclusive collaboration guided by the Retrospectives for Resilience (Figure 8.5). Note that this is not the only retrospective design for this specific topic. This example showcases reinforcing the essential motivators and resilience factors.

Figure 8.5 Retrospectives for Resilience

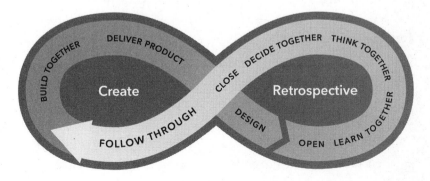

Retrospectives for Resilience
Inspect and Adapt Systems and Teamwork

Scenario

A team's composition included individuals from North America and India. The leader, Alec, observed something disturbing during work interactions: the North America team members were pressing their colleagues from India to create easier names. Alec focused this retrospective on helping build co-intelligence around inclusive collaboration.

Retrospective Logistics

- **Facilitator intent:** Logistics influence the *setting* to ensure that it supports the team's learning. The in-person setting creates an environment of being more *alive*, as *collaborative connections* develop faster in person. Also, being in person fosters leveled engagement across the regions to support healthy *conflict*.
- **Setting:** In person
- **Number of participants:** Invited six
- **Duration:** Three hours (1:00–4:00 p.m.)
- **Day:** Tuesday
- **Food:** Water, soda, coffee, fruit and veggie snacks
- **Location:** On-site medium conference room with lots of windows
- **Setup:** One medium table with room around it for small-group activities; accessory table for supplies, including flip charts, market, sticky notes, and so on.

Retrospective Design

The retrospective design provides a process outline for the facilitator to accomplish the goal.

Set the Stage (20 Minutes)

- **Facilitator intent:** To align on the topic or outcome. To encourage learning, collaboration, and creativity (*alive*).

To model and set the tone for blame-free engagement and increase safety. To provide activities that keep the team's *purpose obvious* by focusing on real work (*fluency*) aspects right from the beginning. To provide activities that help everyone participate immediately and build shared experience and safety (*collaborative connection*).

- **Overall retrospective agenda**
- **Topic:** Increasing inclusion within the team for the best work environment
- **Outcome:** Select one experiment to practice increasing inclusion within the team.
- **Activity:** Pair discussion with this prompt question: "Why is inclusion important to our team?" Each pair puts their one to three answers on separate sticky notes on the large flip chart. This visual information will help center the discussion today on a shared *purpose* when *conflict* arises.
- **Activity:** Revisit the existing team charter for any changes.

Gather Data (25 Minutes)

- **Facilitator intent:** To create safety for exploring this topic with choice on individual contributions (*autonomy*). To increase visibility, internalization, and normalization of the data being shared (*fluency*). To make the whole team experience more *obvious* to everyone and build *co-intelligence* by pulling each team member's perspective on the work so far. To attend to diverse cognitive preferences and needs with a variety of participation techniques (*inclusive collaboration*).
- **Data (5 Minutes):** In this scenario, training on intersectionality and microaggressions has already been done. Display the key concepts.

- **Activity (8 Minutes):** Individual silent writing brainstorming to get examples of where we have and have not exhibited inclusion over the past month.[15] Put each example on the corresponding flip chart.
- **Activity (12 Minutes):** Silently group examples where there are potential connections, duplication, and so on. For ones on which there may be disagreement, provide a consistent way for them to be highlighted (e.g., a sticker).

Break (10 Minutes)

- **Facilitator intent:** Attending to team members' physical and mental needs helps them stay energized and refreshed (*alive*) for the work.
- Encourage healthy choices such as beverages, a quick walk, and so on.

Generate Insights (60 Minutes)

- **Facilitator intent:** To increase internalization of the data positively and concerning fears as a team (*fluency*). To encourage all voices and respectful examination of ideas, impacts, implications, and challenges (*collaborative connection*). To explore the feasibility of new insights and experiments emerging (*co-intelligence* and *obvious*). Staying focused with targeted questions helps momentum (*obvious*). Gathering insights relies on collaborative learning, analysis, internalization, and identification of options (*fluency, co-intelligence,* and healthy *conflict*). As the desired outcome is to get momentum for increasing inclusion, the time allotted is strict (*obvious*).
- **Activity:** Force field analysis exercise to help the group understand what's needed for change.[16] For today's purposes, start with the biggest clusters. Ask, "What is

pushing a change in this?" and "What is restricting this?" Then ask, "What ideas or alternative approaches could be applied here? What new concerns does this raise?" Repeat with another cluster until the allotted time runs out.

Break (10 Minutes)

- **Facilitator intent:** Attending to team members' physical and mental needs helps them stay energized and refreshed (*alive*) for the work.
- Encourage healthy choices such as beverages, a quick walk, and so on.

Decide What to Do (20 Minutes)

- **Facilitator intent:** To ideally converge on the action item that has the most energy and interest (*alive*). Bring the team together to decide the action item to improve the work (*fluency*) that everyone can support (*purpose* and *autonomy*), with equal voices and volunteering encouraging *collaborative connection* and *inclusive collaboration*.
- **Activity:** Criteria board activity to identify and assess decision-making criteria. Brainstorm a list of three to five criteria for making the decision.[17] Place a dot for each idea that you feel meets the criteria for selection. Criteria for this might include "reasonable effort," "valuable impact," "interest or energy," and "willingness to volunteer." Based on the cumulative dots, especially in the volunteer criterion, confirm team agreement on their selection.

Close the Retrospective (5 Minutes)

- **Facilitator intent:** To intentionally remind everyone of the goal and the mindsets required for success, while keeping the activity short (*alive*). To reinforce effective work relationships (*collaborative connection*).

- **Activity:** One-word checkout activity to give participants an opportunity to reflect on their retrospective experience.[18] Use the prompt, "What type of energy will you bring to increase inclusion?"
  Note: This retrospective event was scheduled for three hours. The design accounts for 2 hours and 30 minutes. The additional 30 minutes is buffer time for unexpected adjustments to the design. For example, the group may need more time for a discussion than was planned.

Leadership through learning requires engaging the team to increase inclusive collaborations. In the example retrospective, the specific microaggression remains unaddressed. Because the example observation indicated a lack of co-intelligence and value placed on inclusive collaboration, achieving this retrospective outcome promotes team responsibility to build resiliency around inclusivity.

In this design, Alec included several elements to build a resilient learning team. He *courageously* focused the topic on inclusive collaboration. In each activity, he considered the overall *flow*. The flow of activities orchestrated gradual attention to trust and collaboration (*collaborative connection*), building toward the outcome. Alec started with *compassion* and *courage* to bring awareness of the importance of inclusion immediately. He acknowledged the *complexity* of the topic and kept the focus on creating deep, bounded-time discussions. He invited attendance and invited volunteering to move forward. He expressed *confidence* in the team's ability to move forward together. He ended with a focus on reminding people that how they show up matters for *inclusive collaboration*.

We wish we could tell you that the more you make this a routine, the easier the discussions will be. But we don't want to lie.

There is so much for teams to learn about together. And the only way to gain resiliency is to tackle these difficult inclusion topics in the workplace.

But What If . . . ?

- *We make the situation worse by having the conversation?*
  This is definitely a possibility. People can add other microaggressions when trying to interrupt the original one. Inclusion work is not done overnight, and it is rarely executed perfectly each time. Instead place the importance on being willing to engage and to hear corrections and learn as you embark on making the workplace more inclusive.
- *We infringe on someone's personal space or privacy?*
  People have the right to volunteer what intersectionalities they share and the impacts they have. They also have the right to keep them private. Any sessions about these topics should include a "right to pass" option. Give everyone a choice. You can't demand safety and trust. When interrupting microaggressions, speak only on behalf of yourself, never for others. Speak to the impact that you are experiencing from the microaggression. If it is inappropriate, it should have an impact on you as well.
- *People say this is just "woke" nonsense?*
  Harmful bias and discrimination exist that are hindering collaboration. You must address them to have a healthy workplace. Understand that the person who responds in this manner may be stuck in their learning journey. They may see the world from the perspective of an earlier phase. Share your story about coming down from Mount Stupid. If a team member or colleague persists in this view, consider the future. Learning

leaders need teams to create high-value delivery, which
we get from diverse, inclusive teams. Are they the best
fit, or will they hold the team back?

- *People get canceled?*
People can be willing to learn, even wanting to learn,
but afraid to show their ignorance. The narrative has
been simplified to "a dumb act gets you canceled." Not
true. We all do dumb things on a regular basis at work.
Single microaggressions fall into the category of "dumb
acts we can learn from." In most organizations, you can
effectively address isolated microaggressions without
termination. A person needs to accept the impact and
show a willingness to learn and improve. Yes, viral
stories on social media may increase pressure on organizations. It's unlikely that many organizations termi-
nate people because of one microaggression.

    Intentionally repeated or numerous microaggres-
sions without a willingness to change become aggres-
sions. This is when people are likely to be terminated. If
either of these happen, take the lessons with you and
grow at your next workplace.

Reflections for Your Learning

Begin building the inclusive collaboration resilience factor today.
Learning leaders focus intensely on resilient learning for the
organization, teams, and themselves.

How does DEI influence the choices and decisions in your
organization?

How have you encountered or interrupted workplace
microaggressions?

How do you experience Mount Stupid as a leader?

How could you adapt the example to fit your organization? What similarities and differences would you expose?

How do the Learning Leaders 4Cs (compassion, complexity, confidence, and courage) affect inclusive collaboration?

CHAPTER 9

The Power Dynamics Resilience Factor

Organizational dynamics introduce unspoken power to teams. Power makes a difference in who gets heard, which ideas are followed, and who belongs. Even in the safest of environments, power has influence over engagement. Thus, learning leaders need to mitigate power dynamics (Figure 9.1).

The most acknowledged power is associated with the organizational hierarchy chart and is known as formal or positional power. It carries the option to force action. This is a result of an actual or perceived threat to employment.

Informal power, also known as influential power, derives from prior connections or earned respect for expertise. Informal power encourages action due to admiration or a desire for inclusion or acceptance.

Dominant power represents the norm. This is power that derives from being part of the largest established group. Dominant power encourages action due to momentum that drowns the voices of underrepresented groups.

Finally, everyone has experienced power that affects the team but seems to come from nowhere. They struggle to identify the source. Yet, clearly, some unidentified power sways people, drives actions, and creates impacts.

At any time, everyone is capable of carrying a variety of these powers. Power dynamics may intentionally and unintentionally

Figure 9.1 Power Dynamic Types

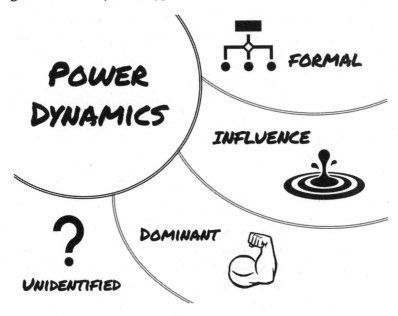

disrupt team resiliency. Power can sway a team's responsibility, purpose, autonomy, co-intelligence, collaborative connections, conflict, and inclusion. Yep, it can disrupt *everything* learning leaders are trying to build.

Su was the newly promoted vice president of marketing. She wanted to gain a better insight into her new teams. She invited herself to each team's retrospective covering the recent marketing campaign rollout. The rollout had been a success. Su was looking forward to building on what the teams had learned.

As she went from retrospective to retrospective, she noticed a few patterns emerging. When she entered each room, she saw that all eyes turned on her and people stopped talking. Team members highlighted specific minor wins. They did express a few of the tougher issues, but always highlighting how these issues were not their fault.

*Afterward, Su talked with the team leaders. She noted,
"I don't understand why they didn't dig deeper into the wins
and challenges they faced in this campaign. The teams pulled
off something major! It was no walk in the park. I know that.
Why didn't they want to tell me about it? Why didn't they
want to build on this success?" Consistently, the leaders
stated, "The team were nervous about being open with you
in the room."*

*Su was immediately a little taken aback with this concern. She
asked, "Why? They should know I am not looking for someone to
blame." Hesitantly, the leaders said, "That's not what they have
experienced in the past." Now, Su felt unfairly treated. She found
herself becoming upset. "Why judge me for my predecessor's
actions? I'm me, and I'm new. They have no reason to assume
they can't be honest with me."*

Given defensive mechanisms, we can understand why Su initially took this personally. She felt she had not done anything wrong. After all, she was new to the job. She was tempted to rationalize and explain how this wasn't fair or professional. But the good news is Su decided to focus on what was most important: becoming a learning leader focused on creating resilient teams. Su got curious and focused on learning what she had missed.

What did she do? By inviting herself, she had established that she didn't need to wait for an invitation to their retrospectives, basically expressing, "I go where and when I want." By participating as an observer, she imposed on the team as if they were performing for their new boss. By staying in the observer role, she prevented any collaboration or connections. By ignoring past experiences and expectations, and by demanding and judging a team event based on meeting her needs, she failed to respectfully meet people where they are. All these combined highlighted that she had power over her teams.

Learning leaders acknowledge the impacts of "power over" dynamics. "Power over" implies using dominance, control, and coercion, even fear-inducing behaviors, to achieve action. When people experience someone wielding power over them, they avoid offering feedback or contributing. They may further go completely silent, not realizing how much the power is influencing their engagement. Even when they do know, talking about a power differential doesn't feel safe. It's too risky. As a result, conflict quickly becomes destructive.

Despite initial defensive reactions, Su knew something was wrong but was confused about what.

Su unpacked her alternatives. She decided to try a different approach to reacting to this feedback and continuing the communication. She used a technique referred to as "2 percent truth." Behind any feedback, there is a kernel of truth. The goal is to find the 2 percent kernel of truth in the feedback.[1] Sometimes the percentage is higher, but there is always at least 2 percent truth to courageously own. You may have to dig deeper and consider systemic conditions that might create negative perceptions and assumptions.

How you respond sets the tone for communication. Let's imagine Su handled the feedback differently.

Consistently, the leaders stated, "The team were nervous being open with you in the room."

Su paused and thought, "What's the 2 percent truth in this statement?"

She paused for longer to let go of the defensive reactions she was having.

She paused for longer to let go of the desire for explanations or more details.

She paused for longer to let go of the desire to justify, explain, or blame.

She asked herself again, "What's the 2 percent truth in this statement?"

Slowly, Su began recognizing truths that contributed to the "power over" dynamic: "I invited myself. My predecessor had led with an iron fist. I do not have connections with these teams. I did not explain my purpose for attending."

Then Su remembered a specific moment. She noted, "Yes, during the go–no-go meeting of the marketing campaign, I asked, 'Are you kidding? How did we not catch that sooner?'" Su was able to find the 2 percent truth of what contributed to people being nervous around her. Now she was tempted again to immediately provide explanations and reasons. But she chose to be curious and silent to invite further communication.

The leaders filled the silence with a variety of responses. Since they felt heard and gained respect for Su's response, they engaged in healthy conflict: "Why were you so upset in the go–no-go meeting?"; "Actually, that's not what freaked my team out. Observing them did"; and "Thank you for acknowledging that. What can we do to improve the situation?"

Learning leaders want delivery of feedback to be clear, specific, respectful, and productive. Yet when you mix power dynamics with conflict, skills disappear. The goal with the 2 percent truth technique is to unlock a small part of the feedback that enables a healthy conflict communication. This technique shows the receiver's willingness to take some responsibility regardless of power. Even if it is a small percentage of the feedback that you can see yourself in and accept, it demonstrates that you are willing to discuss this conflict in a way that neutralizes some of the power imbalance. After sharing the 2 percent truth, silence and curiosity are beneficial. Silence gives space for the other person to ask questions about your response. It may even prompt them to provide more details about the feedback. Find time later in the discussion to explain reasons and assumptions. The important thing to celebrate is that someone is willing to tell you despite the power dynamics.

Learning leaders shift from *power over* others to *power with* others. "Power with" implies using inclusion, collaboration, and participation, as well as supporting behaviors, to achieve action. To embrace a "power with" stance, learning leaders courageously embrace conflicts that may feel like a punch to the gut. They show vulnerability. And they take responsibility for the impact of their power.

By changing her initial defensive response, Su demonstrated "power with" using 2 percent truth. She embraced this conflict by not leveraging her power to dismiss, invalidate, or trivialize the issue. She exhibited respect and a desire to discuss. She showed her willingness to acknowledge the impact of her specific behavior in the go–no-go meeting. She showed vulnerability by acknowledging that she is not perfect and is willing to learn. She gave space, listened, and then engaged in healthy conflict communication. Power dynamics are never absent. But by modeling a growth mindset rather than a focus on blame and shame, Su ensured that the power dynamic was no longer impeding the building of trust and resiliency.

Formal Power

Formal power is the authority one wields based on one's position in an organization. It is also referred to as positional power. It's inescapable. Responsibility over another person's employment and benefits means power. Managers and leaders cause problems when they abuse this power. And it's easy to misuse power over others, or default to it, without realizing. Even good intentions can create significant problems.

Before the retrospective, Derek, the team leader, expressed to the facilitator his frustration. He wanted to move to a new team. He explained that his boss had denied this request because he was too important to the team.

As the retrospective started, the facilitator noticed Derek was the first to speak, and the second, fourth, sixth, and seventh. During the first break, the facilitator challenged him, offering, "Try to have three people speak before you speak."

The retrospective resumed. The facilitator asked a question to the team. Everyone on the team looked at Derek, waiting for him to speak. When he didn't, they kept waiting. He began sweating and looking around uncomfortably. It took several minutes, but eventually someone else cautiously spoke up. The minute they stopped talking, everyone looked at Derek. They were waiting for his reaction and opinion. At that moment, he realized how much he had contributed to this problem.

Toward the end of the retrospective, Derek courageously shared that he had learned a lot about leadership today. He acknowledged that he didn't always have confidence in the team having the answers. And he thought that giving quick answers helped the team be efficient. But thanks to today, he realized that the team was deferring to his leadership position. His "power over" behavior had contributed to unintentionally influencing the team to wait for his opinion before taking action. He was not providing space for the team to collaborate or take responsibility. Thus he wasn't helping the team be efficient or effective. He thanked the facilitator for her intervention.

Formal power is present in explicit organizational hierarchies and implicit hierarchies within teams. Compensation titles highlight seniority, experience, and expectations. For example, an intern is hired onto the team. This intern reports to the manager in the department. A senior person is paired with this intern. The senior person assigns and reviews the intern's workload. Since the senior person has direct influence and impact on workload and employment, they have formal power over the intern.

In any formal power dynamic, people can slip into unhealthy interactions. Managers may attempt to drop this power by saying, "Just consider me one of the team." But this is unrealistic and ignores the complexity of the environment. In a formal power position, you are never just "one of the team." By attempting to make this claim, you create a situation where connections are inauthentic and driven by fear. Responsibility for titles and performance reviews is part of a manager's formal power. So the fear present before engaging is, "If I have conflict with this person, will my career be negatively affected?" This can lead to people holding back their well-reasoned and well-informed ideas. Instead, they choose to defer to those with formal power, justifying this with the thought, "They are in charge and know best."

Learning leaders have compassion for the easily influenced behaviors causing and reacting to "power over" dynamics involving formal power. To be a "power with" learning leader in formal power situations, confront the true risk that justifies behaviors in reaction to "power over" dynamics. If you find yourself feeling the obligation to step in and save the day, ask yourself these questions: What's the risk? What's the risk of having others handle this situation? What's the risk if you step back? Continue to ask, "What's the risk?" in different ways until you uncover the 2 percent truth about what is influencing you that may be hurting the building of resilient learning teams. This helps improve decisions for both the short term and long term, for all involved.

Words of advice:

- With information radiators, make the work visible to promote collaboration and shared responsibility. A service team displayed upcoming work planned. Everyone saw a clearly unequal distribution of challenging work (assigned to those with formal power) and mundane tasks (assigned to those without formal power). Everyone acknowledged that this was not intentional and adjusted the distribution. Now the work plan felt fair. This activity prevented the team from building power dynamic resentments that break resiliency.

- Challenge members with formal positions of authority to learn and consider formal power dynamics. Then ask them to suggest mitigation actions. Options can include not speaking until other people have spoken, being the last to vote, or actively requesting input from others. This helps set expectations and examples about the ideal collaboration within a team.
- As a direct manager, describe the roles you perform on the team in a specific interaction. For example, what roles are you performing in this retrospective? The person with expert information. The manager–decision maker. The facilitator. The observer. Hidden shifts in roles mean team members may not keep up with which influence is intended. To avoid having team members expect or assume one role when you intend another, clarify.
- Be as transparent as possible about how employment impacts are decided. Share the approach to determining promotions, raises, and so on. Provide opportunities for specific feedback related to how performance reviews are assessed and delivered. Transparency will aid in increasing trust and minimize the fears associated with formal power.

Informal Power

When you gain respect in relationships, you gain power to influence others. Both professional and social connections develop based on trust. Respect may form from common interests, expert knowledge, or frequent connections. Informal power, also known as influential power, derives from prior connections or earned respect for expertise. It carries no expectation of acquiescent response or fear of consequences.

People dismiss their ability to intentionally and unintentionally influence others. This happens especially when there is no formal power. Yet informal power can be a more influential dynamic than formal power. In formal power, people may defer to others out of fear of retaliation. In informal power, people may defer to others with the goal of gaining approval. Informal influence is dangerous, as it can build momentum through flattery and acceptance. A prime example of the dangers of informal power comes with the groupthink phenomenon.

In the moment, groupthink can seem productive. It's not. It does not tap into the wisdom of the team. Inauthentic harmony does not benefit the customer, organization, teams, or people.

A team was in a high-pressure situation for delivery, so they decided that taking time to reflect in a retrospective would pay off in saved time later. Two people from other projects expressed interest in attending the retrospective. They had no formal authority over this department and team. They wanted to attend because they thought

---

Groupthink is a psychological phenomenon that occurs within a group of people in which the desire for harmony or conformity in the group results in an irrational or dysfunctional decision-making outcome. Cohesiveness, or the desire for cohesiveness, in a group may produce a tendency among its members to agree at all costs. It arises from the need to belong to the team, the network, or the clique with influence.[2]

*they could learn from the team's experiences. The team re-
spected these two individuals for their expert knowledge and
contributions to the company. Yet there was concern.*

*The facilitator held a side conversation with the two individu-
als. The discussion covered the benefits of their observation and
the potential informal power risks. The two individuals understood and agreed to the facilitator's plan for neutralizing the risk.*

*At the start of the retrospective, the facilitator invited the team
to choose working agreements. The facilitator described three
retrospective roles (facilitator, participants, and observers).
Attendees could change roles, but they had to be explicit with the
change. At any point, any team member could question if someone had changed roles without being explicit. The two outsiders
accepted their role as observers.*

*Later in the retrospective, one of the outsiders started trying to
solve a team-level issue. Many team members started quickly
agreeing with everything the outsider said. The collaboration
ceased. The team shifted to groupthink through the influence of
informal power.*

*Luckily, this team was building resiliency. One team member
asked if the outsider wanted to change roles and become a participant. The outsider apologized and declined to change roles. The
team returned to questioning and collaborating to find a solution.*

*At the close of the retrospective, the outsider sought out that team
member. The outsider offered them an appreciation for speaking up
in a difficult situation. The outsider acknowledged that his comments had started an unproductive tangent. He had begun problem
solving without all the information. He saw they eventually arrived
at a much better solution than the one he was thinking about. He
apologized for leaving his role and derailing the team.*

If left unchecked, informal power can slowly build serious consequences. Informal power can easily be justified by, "They are

smart! That is a great idea!" But it ignores inclusive collaboration and embracing conflict. Over time, people feel like games or popularity contests are being played with the important people at work—not to mention the poor outcomes for the customer. This facilitator created a safe setting where "power over" influences could be highlighted and mitigated. They had confidence in the team's co-intelligence to notice their influence quickly and in their willingness to raise the question.

Learning leaders help grow everyone's informal power. It can be helpful to teams when using "power with" dynamics. Informal power gives others access to a beneficial network of people and information. It's not a limited resource. It arises from a variety of sources and networks. Highlight the ways your colleagues have access and gain value from different connections. Ask team members about their strengths, expertise, and connections. Then increase the number of people giving advice in the team. Foster new connections to expanding networks.

Words of advice:

- Keep the focus on the benefits of collaborating toward results rather than fake harmony. Embrace conflict as a healthy means to creativity and innovation, while ensuring that all voices are being heard and engaged.
- Challenge the informal power holders among team members. Holders acknowledge and share their influence. Be transparent and intentional about when and how you engage with others. For example, are you the first to provide an idea, or do you give space for other ideas first? This will create a balance within the team power dynamics.
- Limit bottlenecks and increase transparency in the work system. When only one team member has information or

skills, it creates informal power and a single point of failure. Focus on building co-intelligence in the team.

- Reach out to stakeholders. They can apply their formal and informal power to support the team outcomes. Customers and businesspeople can help teams expand informal power outside the team. When everyone recognizes they have a shared focus on the same goal, they are more likely to work together.

Dominant Power

Dominant power represents the norm. This is power that derives from being part of the largest established group within an intersectionality. The dominant power group maintains this power knowingly or unknowingly. And those who are not within the dominant power group are underrepresented.

Too often, when individuals attempt to discuss the "power over" impact of dominant power, others silence them or, worse, blame them for not supporting the dominant group. They may get labeled as "not a team player." Silencing any member of the team makes the dominant power dangerous. Achieving inclusive collaboration relies on the dominant creating space for the underrepresented.

Fran was the lead on a remote team with nine men and one woman. Seven team members worked at a co-located office in Boston. Three worked at home in different Colorado cities.

One day, the woman spoke up about other team members consistently expecting her to take notes. She said, "I was happy to be a good sport about it and go first, but now it seems you assume that I'll take notes every time. That doesn't seem fair. Who else can take notes this time?" She expected that one of the men would volunteer. Instead, one said, "But you have the best skills with the online whiteboard. Your sketch notes make our meeting minutes more artistic. Women always have the best handwriting; I guess that must extend to online tools too." Several other men nodded in agreement. Still, none of them offered to take notes. Not feeling safe to address the statements directly, she tried once more to focus on the request: "I'd really like someone else to take a turn for this meeting. Everyone can benefit from practicing on the online whiteboard." Still no one spoke up. Another team member said, "C'mon, just do it. Maybe one of us will volunteer next time. None of us are prepared today." She gave up the discussion. She took minimal notes, trying to make a point that no one noticed. She felt excluded and upset by the dominant power in the team. And no one else volunteered at the next meeting.

Later that month, the team discussed the schedule for their regular team meetings. They held a daily meeting for quick coordination. They had longer meetings biweekly to explore and plan upcoming work. They held a retrospective monthly. They needed to schedule the meetings for the next quarter. A team member from Boston suggested that they should start the full-day retrospective at 9:00 a.m. They assumed it was reasonable because no one in Colorado commuted and anything later meant that Boston people's commute home would increase by two hours due to rush hour. All the team members from Boston agreed. "Wait a minute," one of the Colorado-based people spoke up. "That's 7:00 a.m. in my time zone! I do my exercises and then have to help with getting my kids ready for online school. I don't want to start that early." One of the other Coloradans agreed. The other was out sick that day. The proposer of the time said, "I'm sure you could figure something out. Let's vote on it! Roman voting—thumbs up if you agree, thumbs down if you don't, and thumbs sideways if you'll support whatever the team decides. Majority rules are fair." They voted and got the obvious outcome: the start time was 9:00 a.m. eastern time. As a result, one of the Colorado team members always showed up late to the retrospectives.

In each of these scenarios, the underrepresented participants encountered dominant "power over" dynamics. The team composition may have increased diversity but was not focused on inclusive collaboration. In addition to inclusivity needs, dominant "power over" dynamics continue to emerge frequently in the workplace because humans need to belong.

An in-group is a group to which a person psychologically identifies themselves as belonging. By contrast, an out-group is a group with which an individual does not identify or belong. These groups can align with various intersectionalities. The underrepresented will experience out-group association. In the first story in this section, the woman was facing gender bias as the justification for her colleagues' behavior. In the second story, there were fewer people from the Colorado location on the team.

Experiencing out-group association can have serious impacts for building resilient learning teams. The in-group is the expected norm. This perpetuates an atmosphere where dominant power groups remained unaware of any impacts. Thus, historically, underrepresented groups are expected to "step up," "not be so sensitive," and "get along." In the first example, the woman's request was dismissed. Instead, she received microaggressions as a response. In the second example, the perspectives of the people from Colorado were trivialized. They were not given a chance to provide an alternative idea. Dominant "power over" dynamics pressure the underrepresented to "go with the flow" or risk not belonging on the team.

Learning leaders leverage "power with" dynamics by providing balance. They advocate for the voices of underrepresented team members. They can challenge the dominant in-group to amplify underrepresented perspectives. They can highlight instances of privilege. They invite underrepresented voices early into discussions. They facilitate and distribute learning opportunities equitably. They initiate discussions about the importance of minimizing bias and microaggressions. These are complex topics. It can take courage to go against the dominant flow. Learning leaders show compassion in recognizing the difficulty that dominant groups may have with changing their behaviors, while insisting that change must occur.

Words of advice:

- Increase diversity within the team. The more diversity, the more the whole team will realize the need for equal say. Dominant power will lose its ability to suppress alternate views.
- Sponsor training to increase DEI awareness and encourage behavioral changes. This is not a one-course or one-time training. There are several aspects to it, and significant practice is required. Participating in building co-intelligence is beneficial in itself, heightening the consciousness of the physical and emotional needs of the whole team.
- Expand the working agreement and team charter. Create agreements beforehand. Include an active discussion about how each team member would raise dominant power and inclusion concerns. For example, "We allow each other to finish sentences before speaking. We will raise the team mascot to give a visual that we are not giving each other space."

Unidentified Power

The previously discussed powers are typically easy to identify and understand. We can dampen or amplify the impacts. Then there is power that has effects on the team but whose source is not known. Unidentified power tends to fall into one of two categories.

One is closely related to intentional hidden agendas. This may result from a desire for secrecy among individuals hoping to accomplish an objective. The other area is an unintended side consequence of a seemingly unrelated decision. Unidentified power is present when we cannot immediately trace the source, yet clearly some unidentified force is influencing the team and results.

Unidentified power is at play with hidden agendas, secrecy, or manipulation.

> *Recently, Bonnie switched teams. One of the main reasons for this switch was a destructive conflict with another team member, Sam. Bonnie couldn't stand him. In Bonnie's opinion, he was dangerous for the organization due to his incompetence.*
>
> *Bonnie went to lunch with Srinivasa, a new teammate. During their lunch, Bonnie learned that Srinivasa was dating Bonnie's replacement on the previous team. Feeling protective of Srinivasa and this new person, Bonnie began giving warnings and advice, always followed with an expectation that it was confidential information and that Srinivasa should not share the source. Bonnie indicated that she would be willing to help behind the scenes.*

As you can imagine, this did not go well for anyone involved. Sam and Ritu struggled to connect. Yet every attempt to understand the distrust was challenging. Ritu refused to identify her boyfriend, Srinivasa, as the "telephone game" source. She didn't know about Bonnie's involvement. Eventually, the impacts on that team rippled back to creating impacts between Bonnie and Srinivasa. Although Bonnie started out trying to be helpful, the 2 percent truth was that she also didn't want Sam to be successful. Some of Bonnie's information was very biased and opinionated, not based in fact. She was creating unidentified "power over" dynamics.

Unidentified power may also arise as an unintended side consequence of a seemingly unrelated decision.

The Dynamo team complained to their team leader about an impediment to their work. They had accepted responsibility to achieve the team's purpose. But as they worked toward the outcome, they stalled. The Dynamos wanted to move forward but couldn't. Their work depended on cooperation with other teams in a different department. Yet the other teams didn't recognize discussing and collaborating on the data as their current priority.

When the Dynamo team leader brought it up with the other teams' leaders, it didn't go well. They didn't see the difficulty. The teams had provided a document of the data. Teams were receiving different priorities based on whom the team reported to. And they were working on the right priorities set for their teams. The Dynamos were told, "This is how it has always been. Deal with it."

The Dynamo team was experiencing unidentified power that lacked ownership. The team now had a choice: miss the deadline, or develop something they had control over, even if it meant duplication within the organization.

There was no leader in this organization creating a reporting chart with the intent of causing barriers to success. Leaders made decisions that had unintended consequences that were difficult to identify and own. When it comes to unidentified power, people may sense that they are in a conflict with an amorphous adversary. People know something is off but can't figure it out. This elicits people's knee-jerk, fear-based, self-protective responses.

Without radical transparency, the source of power stays unrevealed. Radical transparency counteracts "power over" dynamics.[3] Greater visibility reduces the chance for doubts and assumptions to arise. Learning leaders courageously employ "power with" dynamics by shining a spotlight on the elephant in the room. They build awareness of the complex system of undiscussables and unknowns. We don't have to know what invited the "elephant," but we don't have to ignore it either. Bringing attention to the impacts may help identify unidentified power sources. Resilient learning teams acknowledge the complexity of the situation and learn their way forward.

Words of advice:
- Identify all the stakeholders involved. Also brainstorm key advisers who could benefit the work. They may have a wider view. Reflect continuously and be explicit about these participants. It will reduce the emergence of alternative, more dubious ways of providing information.
- Acknowledge that there will always be factors we don't know about. There are always issues beyond our control. Seek ways to mitigate the impacts and bring these instances into transparent discussion.
- Keep the team focused on learning forward. Resilience is about handling the unexpected and the unknown. Treat these power conflicts the same way—learn through them.

Example Design

Leaders encourage their teams to become resilient learning teams by highlighting underlying challenges, not once but continuously along the way. They invite the team to use a retrospective to explore specific topics. As a leader, you don't get to decide what the team's outcome action items are. Yet you can choose to focus on the area where you've observed the team is struggling. The retrospective example given here showcases how teams focus on minimizing power dynamics guided by the Retrospectives for Re-

Figure 9.2 Retrospectives for Resilience

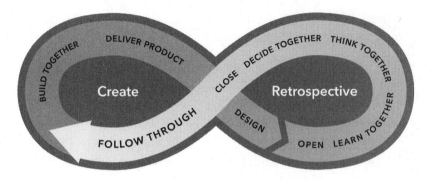

silence (Figure 9.2). Note that this is not the only retrospective design for this specific topic.

Scenario

Review the story about Su at the beginning of this chapter. Remember that the new vice president found help from the 2 percent truth exercise. After her experience, Su wanted to minimize power dynamics within the whole team. This is the retrospective design.

Retrospective Logistics

- **Facilitator intent:** Logistics influence the *setting* to ensure that it supports the team's learning
- **Setting:** Online—video
- **Number of participants:** Invited 12
- **Duration:** Full day (9:00 a.m.–4:30 p.m. with 12:00–1:00 p.m. lunch break)
- **Day:** Wednesday
- **Food:** NA
- **Location:** Remote

- **Setup:** Videoconference tool and remote collaboration tool
- **Facilitator:** Su hired an external, neutral facilitator.

Retrospective Design

The retrospective design provides a process outline for the facilitator to accomplish the goal.

Set the Stage (30 Minutes)

- **Facilitator intent:** To align on the topic or outcome. To encourage learning, collaboration, and creativity (*alive*). To model and set the tone for blame-free engagement and increase safety by leveling the *power dynamics*. The activities keep the team's *purpose obvious* by focusing on real work (*fluency*) right from the beginning. The activities help everyone participate immediately and build shared experience (*inclusive collaboration* and *collaborative connection*).
- **Overall retrospective agenda**
- **Topic:** Transitioning to "power with" dynamics
- **Outcome:** Define one action for up to three power dynamics that will help the team engage "power with" rather than "power over" dynamics.
- **Activity:** Revisit the existing team charter for any changes.
- **Activity:** Analyze cartoon exercise. Choose a cartoon that highlights power dynamics (Dilbert tends to have excellent options for this topic). Use the following prompts: "Does this reflect our reality? What assumptions, organization actions, or personal behaviors contribute to it? Why is this description mostly targeted at managers? What are we losing by simply

accepting this 'power over' or control narrative?" With different prompts, vary the participation approach to include individual answers, small-group discussions, and large-group discussions.

Gather Data (20 Minutes)

- **Facilitator intent:** To create safety for exploring this topic with choice on individual contributions (*autonomy*). To increase visibility, internalization, and normalization of the data being shared (*fluency*). To make the whole team experience more *obvious* to everyone and build *co-intelligence* by pulling each team member's perspective on the work so far. To attend to diverse cognitive preferences and needs with a variety of participation techniques (*inclusive collaboration*) that demonstrate that *conflict* and *power* grow if not transparent.
- **Data:** Before the retrospective, as prework, the facilitator sent each participant a PDF with generic descriptions of team power dynamics. The facilitator asked them to bring their notes about where they observe and experience these dynamics in their workplace.
- **Activity:** "What's in it for" wheel on online whiteboard tool (Figure 9.3). For each power dynamic, everyone uses sticky notes to post their perception of what's in it for (i.e., benefits to) the various sections.

Break (15 Minutes)

- **Facilitator intent:** Attending to team members' physical and mental needs helps them stay energized and refreshed (*alive*) for the work.
- Encourage healthy choices such as beverages, a quick walk, and so on.

Figure 9.3 "What's in It for" Wheel Example

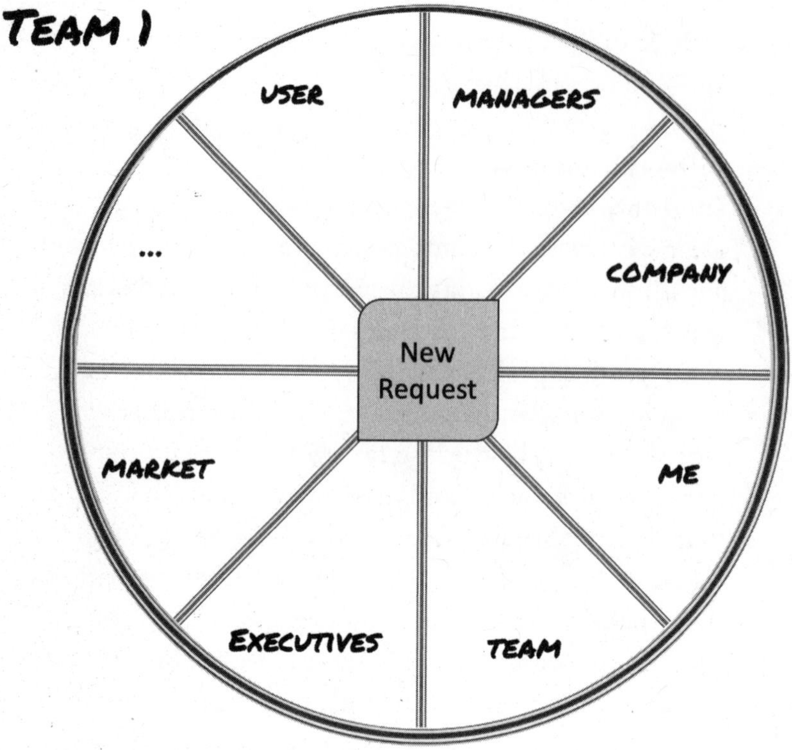

Gather Data (90 Minutes)—Explore the Territory

- **Facilitator intent:** To create safety for exploring this
  topic with choice on individual contributions (*autonomy*). To increase visibility, internalization, and normalization of the data being shared. To make the whole
  team experience more *obvious* to everyone and build
  co-intelligence by pulling each team member's perspective
  on the work so far. To attend to diverse cognitive
  preferences and needs with a variety of participation
  techniques (*inclusive collaboration*) that demonstrate that
  conflict grows if not transparent. To emphasize that

human interaction is complex and that *"power* over" dynamics grow if they are unexamined.

- **Activity:** Acknowledging the elephant. On the virtual collaboration board, draw four columns—one representing each power dynamic—and a picture of an elephant. For each column, put sticky notes of the information created during the prework. Instruct people to write the behavior, situation, or role (no names) and impact. The "and impact" part creates vulnerability for all. Allow time for people to absorb what was listed. In triads, each group chooses one of the power dynamics to focus on. In virtual triad breakouts, create affinity groups for similar sticky notes. Discuss whether this dynamic is a symptom of something else or the most influential elephant. Discuss what things cause people to make, or avoid making, a power play. Discuss each candidate for most influential power dynamic elephant with the whole team. A volunteer from each triad shares their candidate.

Lunch (60 Minutes)

Encourage team members to take a refreshing break as well as eating their meal. Take a walk. Get away from the screen in virtual meetings. Come back with their thinking and bodies refreshed.

Generate Insights (30 Minutes)—Build Listening and Empathy

- **Facilitator intent:** To build empathy and open minds to where intentions and impacts are not always aligned. To increase internalization of the data positively and concerning fears as a team (*fluency*). Encourage all voices and respectful examination of ideas, impacts, implications, and challenges (*collaborative connection* and

inclusive collaboration). Explore the feasibility of new
insights and experiments emerging (*co-intelligence* and
fluency). Staying focused with targeted questions helps
momentum (*obvious*). Gathering insights relies on
collaborative learning, analysis, and the identification
of options (building *co-intelligence* and healthy *conflict*).

- **Activity:** As any power dynamic requires involvement
from more than one person, what are the various roles
within each of the four elephant candidates shared? In
pairs, determine the 2 percent truth of your contribution to these elephants. In a whole-group debrief,
discuss, "Why do we need to acknowledge both the
intent and the impact of these elephants?"

Generate Insights (50 Minutes)—Examine the Impact

- **Facilitator intent:** To foster shared responsibility of
impacts by allowing space for individual thought,
collaborative interactions, creative exploration, varied
opinions, and acknowledgment of *complexity* (*inclusive
connection*). To increase the internalization of the data
positively and concerning fears as a team (*fluency*). To
encourage all voices and respectful examination of
ideas, impacts, implications, and challenges (*collaborative connection*). To explore the feasibility of new insights
and experiments emerging (*co-intelligence* and *fluency*).
Staying focused with targeted questions helps momentum (*obvious*). Gathering insights relies on collaborative
learning, analysis, and identification of options (building *co-intelligence* and healthy *conflict*). As the team sees
options for action, pay attention to how each will affect
power dynamics.

- **Activity:** Constellation activity helps to determine
team member's various interests for resolving the

impacts of power dynamics.[4] For the four candidate elephants, use the constellation to facilitate examining the impact and interest. The following are some example engagement prompts: "What's the risk if addressed or unaddressed?" "What are the short- or long-term benefits?" As conflict arises, use prompts such as, "What would need to be true for you to move to a higher interest?" and "What else needs to be heard?"

Break (10 Minutes)

- **Facilitator intent:** Attending to team members' physical and mental needs helps them stay energized and refreshed (*alive*) for the work.
- Encourage healthy choices such as beverages, a quick walk, and so on.

Generate Insights (60 Minutes)—Ideas

- **Facilitator intent:** To foster shared responsibility for impacts by allowing space for individual thought, collaborative interactions, creative exploration, varied opinions, and acknowledgment of *complexity* (*inclusive connection*). To increase the internalization of the data positively and concerning fears as a team (*fluency*). To encourage all voices and respectful examination of ideas, impacts, implications, and challenges (*collaborative connection*). To explore the feasibility of new insights and experiments emerging (*co-intelligence* and *fluency*). Staying focused with targeted questions helps momentum (*obvious*). Gathering insights relies on collaborative learning, analysis, and identification of options (building *co-intelligence* and healthy *conflict*). As the team sees options for action, pay attention to how each will affect *power dynamics*.

- **Activity:** With the elephants that had majority high interest, begin forming "power with" ideas. In triads, create an experiment that would be a countermeasure to one of the high-interest elephants. Discover ideas that will help the team engage "power with" rather than "power over" dynamics. Have a volunteer from each triad share their experiment idea with the whole group. Then, for each experiment noted, try these new questions within the constellation: "How much control do we have? What is your interest level if selected?" As conflict arises, use prompts such as, "How could we adjust the experiment to make it acceptable?"

Break (10 Minutes)

- **Facilitator intent:** Attending to team members' physical and mental needs helps them stay energized and refreshed (*alive*) for the work.
- Encourage healthy choices such as beverages, a quick walk, and so on.

Decide What to Do (40 Minutes)

- **Facilitator intent:** To ideally converge on the action items that have the most energy and interest (*alive*). To bring the team together to decide the action item to improve the work (*fluency*) that everyone can support (*purpose*) (*autonomy*), with equal voices and volunteering encouraging *collaborative connection* and *inclusive collaboration*. Ensure that "power with" *dynamics* influence team choices.
- **Activity:** In the Fist of Five activity, participants use a hand signal to indicate their level of agreement with a proposal. Holding up five fingers shows high, enthusiastic agreements, while holding up one finger indicates

high disagreement that will veto the proposal. Use it to identify the proposed experiments that generate the most energy from team members.[5] Then request two volunteers to lead the experiment with the most energy shown. The experiments that get volunteers are the chosen ones, with a maximum of three experiments to minimize change fatigue.

- **Activity:** Create an initial transparent plan of moving forward with the focus results.

Close the Retrospective (20 Minutes)

- **Facilitator intent:** To intentionally take time to acknowledge and encourage others as we move forward (*alive*). To receive feedback for the facilitator. To reinforce effective work relationships (*collaborative connection* and *inclusive collaboration*) toward shared team *purpose*.
- **Communicate location of transparency plan**
- **Activity:** Each individual fills out a survey form for the external facilitator.
- **Activity:** One person conveys a specific appreciation to a partner. The only response is "thank you." Then switch. Complete two rounds of appreciation. Then, until the facilitator calls time, repeat with new partners.
  Note: This retrospective event was scheduled for six and a half hours, not including lunch. The design accounts for 6 hours and 15 minutes. The additional 15 minutes is buffer time for unexpected adjustments to the design. For example, the group may need more time for a discussion than was planned.

Learning leaders *courageously* model transparent power dynamics. In this retrospective design, the *flow* of activities required continuous attention to safety and neutralizing *power dynamics* (while talking about power dynamics) to achieve its *purpose*. The facilitator started with *compassion* by acknowledging the need to address power dynamics in the team. They demonstrated *confidence* in the team's ability to embrace healthy conflict and gave space for building inclusive collaborative connections. The facilitator tapped into the team's *co-intelligence* to discover experiments. They provided people with opportunities to highlight *complexity* in the team decisions. They ended by celebrating and appreciating the collaboration within the team.

Learning through leadership requires accepting that power issues will repeatedly emerge in new and different ways. Learning leaders emphasize reducing power dynamics. They shine a spotlight on the impacts. They make everything visible and normalized. They keep the first set of actions small, easy, and not very threatening. And they attend to everyone's psychological safety. The approach to "power with" dynamics is about a desire to positively challenge each other. With each retrospective that reinforces "power with" dynamics, learning leaders help the team build resiliency.

But What If . . . ?

- *The manager likes their power over others?*
  The 2 percent truth is that managers, who have formal power, experience an enormous amount of pressure. Pressure for resolution builds high stress, which leads to bad behaviors. What if they don't care about power? Leaders can mistake efficiency for effectiveness. Instead, emphasize that everyone has the shared goal of finding solutions.
- *The senior analyst keeps taking control of everything?*
  The 2 percent truth is that the senior analyst, who has informal power, wants to do a good job. People may

attempt to justify "power over" dynamics by saying, "I didn't have a choice. I had to step in and save this for the customer." People are right to step in when a decision could destroy an entire organization—for example, an illegal tax decision. Or when physical harm to others might happen. That said, this heroic mode is short-sighted and misused. By flexing power over others to make fast decisions, the individual reduces the team's shared responsibility. Each time this happens, we affect resiliency and lessen the organization's ability to scale productivity. People tend to focus on short-term reasons to negate team collaboration. This rarely produces either short-term or long-term effective results. Instead, dig in deeper to what is motivating this individual to seize control. Encourage the sharing of experiences through step-by-step stories about how behavior affects others. Create spaces where collaboration across informal power dynamics happens.

- *The dominant subgroup keeps making decisions separately from the whole group?*
  The 2 percent truth is that people with dominant power focus on making progress just like anyone else. They are not always aware of their exclusiveness. To start, assume that it wasn't planned—the discussion unexpectedly happened, and when an idea strikes, they go for it! If there is good intent, then we can focus on co-intelligence. Fast does not always produce effectiveness, especially if people are being excluded. To achieve shared responsibility, the team has to be part of the decision. Discuss together, "What could be the longer-lasting negative impacts on the team if this keeps happening?"

- *Team members will not shine a spotlight on the elephant?*
  The 2 percent truth is that people experiencing unidentified power are nervous. When we don't know how the
  situation formed, we wait, mainly out of fear of making
  things worse. Or naming the problem may have back-
  fired in the past. Unidentified power gains momentum
  because avoidance is a form of protection. Examine
  alternatives that increase the safety and transparency
  in the team. Ask, "How can we discuss the issue of
  systemic effects rather than blaming specific people?
  How can we focus on an identifiable, smaller part of the
  elephant to find a solution? How can we support the
  team members better in conflict?"

Reflections for Your Learning

Begin minimizing the power dynamics resilience factor today.
Learning leaders focus intensely on resilient learning for the
organization, teams, and themselves.

How have you experienced the impact of formal power in
  your organization?
How has informal power influenced decisions in your
  organization?
How have dominant power dynamics created inequities in
  your organization?
When has an unidentified power dynamic changed an
  outcome?
How could you adapt the example to fit your organization? What similarities and differences would you
  expose?
How do the Learning Leaders 4Cs (compassion, complexity, confidence, and courage) affect power dynamics?

Conclusion
Where Do You Go from Here?

Purpose and autonomy without co-intelligence creates subpar quality.

Purpose and co-intelligence without autonomy equals dependencies and bottlenecks.

Co-intelligence and autonomy with no purpose means we do things for the sake of doing things.

All three are essential.

Engaging collaborative connections means greater trust.

Building inclusive collaboration means greater wisdom.

Encouraging healthy conflict means greater creativity.

Being transparent about power dynamics means greater engagement.

Taken together, all four produce resilient teams.

magine a world where learning leaders are the norm. Where resilient learning teams thrive. Where you make a difference for yourself, others, and your organization.

What if you experienced helping people learn? For example, "I really do appreciate your help building our team relationships and especially the time you've taken with me. I've got opportunities for growth. You're helping me not only identify them, but figure out how to approach the changes I need to make. You have helped change my career and my life. I'm at a point where I feel impostor syndrome leaving and I am much more fulfilled in what I do" (feedback given to a learning leader).

What if you received feedback about helping the team succeed? For example, "You gave us as team members the context behind the goals so that we understood why they were important to the company and how they were making the company better" (feedback given to a learning leader).

What if you saw your influence on team resilience? For example, "We've talked longer about this than it would take for us just to experiment together. We know change can be hard, but I know that we'll figure it out. *(Long pause.)* Can you believe that we are now more uncomfortable when things are not changing?" (team discussion overheard by a learning leader).

What if you had the chance to influence others' journey to leadership through learning? For example, an engineering manager had a lot of tasks to do to create a setting for new teams. HR reached out with an offer of a budget to plan a year-end celebration for every team. He couldn't add this to his pile of work. So, in the next team meeting, the leader asked which team members were interested in planning how best to use the funds. Team members volunteered. In a surprising move, the funding tripled. Everyone thought a larger amount might mean the leader would take back the planning. The manager shrugged and said, "The amount doesn't matter. [Team members] will learn about how to interact with company bureaucracy. They'll discover what other team members value. It will build their sense of autonomy. It offers a chance to lead. It's so worth it for the learning." Team members eagerly accepted the opportunity to make decisions for the team. (Story shared by a learning leader.)

What if you saw a chance to inspire your organization? For example, "In my current company, we have some really institutionalized command-and-control leadership models. I see a lot of well-liked, well-intentioned managers who don't understand how to effectively manage a team and not continually undermine it. I'm part of [an internal leadership team] that's actively working to dismantle that. We know it can be better" (intention shared by a learning leader).

What if you could say and mean, "I love my work. I have the best job ever"?

Resilient Learning Teams

Leadership through learning reflects the leader's role in growing team resilience to discover long-lasting value. To go from imagination to reality, learning leaders build resilient learning teams (Figure 10.1).

Resilience is the human ability to meet and recover from adversity and setbacks. Resilient learning teams have the ability to sustain under pressure and chaos. They emphasize shared responsibility to respond to emergent conditions. They welcome and celebrate complex problems. They enable long-lasting business agility by anticipating and responding to changing realities.

Resilient learning team members form a collaborating, self-organizing team. They have a shared, meaningful purpose. They have the autonomy to determine how they approach the work. They amplify the value of co-intelligence through continuous learning together. They consistently build trusting connections

Figure 10.1 Leadership through Learning

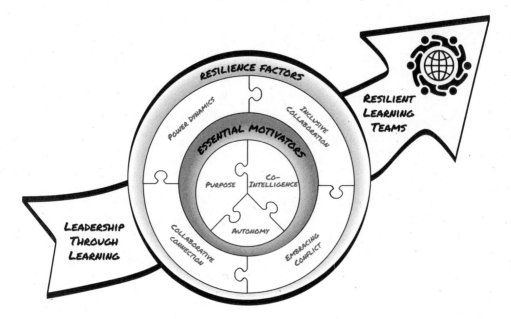

to challenge themselves and others. They proactively increase their diversity and inclusion. They pursue healthy conflict as a path to creativity and innovation. They encourage "power with" dynamics for greater effectiveness.

When people learn together, they grow together. When they grow together, they share responsibility together. When they share responsibility, there's no value in blame.

Part One Reflection

Leaders are not responsible for the results, leaders are responsible for the people who are responsible for the results. And the best way to drive performance in an organization is to create an environment in

which information can flow freely, mistakes can be highlighted and help can be offered and received.
—*Simon Sinek, The Infinite Game[1]*

Begin strengthening the essential motivators in your teams today. Using questions aligned with the techniques described in *The Art of Focused Conversation*, reflect on these questions in your world.[2]

What have you seen that exemplifies the essential motivators?

What have people said about learning or leadership that sticks with you?

What unexpected ideas challenged how you felt?

What are you hesitant to consider?

What are you excited about trying?

How are the essential motivators important to your teams?

What does leadership through learning mean for you?

What might it entail to step away from blaming?

What actions could you take to increase purpose, autonomy, and co-intelligence?

What do you need to do differently to incorporate the Learning Leaders 4Cs?

Part Two Reflection

Resilience is not about overcoming, but becoming.
—*Sherri Mandell, American author[3]*

Begin cultivating the resilience factors in your teams today. Using questions aligned with *The Art of Focused Conversation*, reflect on these questions in your world.

> What have you seen that exemplifies the resilience factors?
> What have people said about effective teams that sticks with you?
> What unexpected ideas challenged how you felt?
> What are you hesitant to consider?
> What are you excited about trying?
> How are the resilience factors important to your teams?
> What does trust mean for you?
> How do the resilience factors lessen blame?
> What actions could you take to address collaborative connection, inclusive collaboration, conflict, and power dynamics?
> What do you need to do differently to incorporate resilience factors for teams you lead or belong to?

Final Reflection

Leaders intend to make a positive difference. Yet leadership roles challenge us to create the setting for followers to succeed, which isn't easy. And being a learning leader is difficult. No two journeys of leadership through learning follow exactly the same path. The only wrong step to take is to never take a step. We have the confidence that you will keep learning how to break free of blame and build resiliency. We can't wait to hear your stories.

> How will you embrace compassion for your own learning as well as your teams'?

How will you grow and demonstrate confidence in your teams' ability to learn?

How will you accept and dance with complexity as your teams grow?

How will you courageously lead without blame?

Notes

Preface

1. Diana Larsen and Tricia Broderick, "Blaming is NOT Accountability," Agile 2021 conference, July 20, 2021, www.agilealliance.org /agile2021.

2. From Dave Snowden and Riva Greenberg, *Cynefin—Weaving Sense-Making into the Fabric of Our World* (Singapore: Cognitive Edge—The Cynefin Co., 2020).

Chapter 1

1. Daniel Kahneman, *Thinking Fast and Slow* (New York: Farrar, Straus and Giroux, 2011). Also see "Why Our Minds Swap Out Hard Questions for Easy Ones," MIT Sloan Management Review, December 22, 2011, https://sloanreview.mit.edu/article/why-our-minds-swap-out-hard -questions-for-easy-ones/.

2. Peter Drucker, "Knowledge-Worker Productivity: The Biggest Challenge," *California Management Review* 41, no. 2 (1999): 79–94. doi:10.2307/41165987.

3. Steve Denning, "The Dumbest Idea in the World: Maximizing Shareholder Value," *Forbes*, November 28, 2011, https://www.forbes.com /sites/stevedenning/2011/11/28/maximizing-shareholder-value-the -dumbest-idea-in-the-world/?sh=354420822870.

4. Evan Leybourn and Shane Hastie, *#noprojects: A Culture of Continuous Value* (lulu.com, 2019).

5. Mary Lynn Manns and Linda Rising, *Fearless Change: Patterns for Introducing New Ideas* (Boston: Addison-Wesley Professional, 2015); Esther Derby, *7 Rules for Positive, Productive Change: Micro Shifts, Macro Results* (Oakland, CA: Berrett-Koehler, 2019).

6. Chip R. Bell, "Great Leaders Learn Out Loud," American Management Association, January 24, 2019, https://www.amanet.org/articles/great-leaders-learn-out-loud/.

7. David Snowden and Riva Greenberg, *Cynefin: Weaving Sense-Making into the Fabric of Our World* (Singapore: Cognitive Edge—The Cynefin Co., 2020).

8. Agile Alliance homepage, accessed April 15, 2022, https://www.agilealliance.org/glossary/business-agility.

9. Nathan Bennett and G. James Lemoine, "What VUCA Really Means for You," *Harvard Business Review*, January–February 2014, https://hbr.org/2014/01/what-vuca-really-means-for-you.

10. Peter M. Senge, *The Fifth Discipline: The Art & Practice of The Learning Organization* (New York: Currency, 2006).

Part One

1. Daniel H. Pink, *Drive: The Surprising Truth about What Motivates Us* (New York: Riverhead Books, 2009).

2. David Marquet, in *Turn the Ship Around!*, has similar elements of control, competence, and clarity. L. David Marquet, *Turn the Ship Around! A True Story of Turning Followers into Leaders* (New York: Portfolio, 2013).

Chapter 2

1. Peter Drucker, in Forbes Quotes: Thoughts on the Business of Life, https://www.forbes.com/quotes/7416/.

2. "Frontline Leader Project," DDI, accessed March 8, 2022, https://www.ddiworld.com/research/frontline-leader-project.

3. Francis Ford Coppola, dir., *The Godfather* (Paramount Pictures, 1972).

4. Kent Beck, "Accountability in Software Development," Medium, December 1, 2021, https://medium.com/@kentbeck_7670/accountability-in-software-development-375d42932813.

5. Stephen R. Covey, *The 7 Habits of Highly Effective People: Powerful Lessons in Personal Change* (New York: Free Press, 2004).

6. Christopher Avery, *The Responsibility Process: Unlocking Your Natural Ability to Live and Lead with Power* (Pflugerville, TX: Partnerwerks, 2016).

7. Max Nisen and John Allspaw, "Why Etsy Engineers Send Company-Wide Emails Confessing Mistakes They Made," Quartz, September 18,

2015, https://qz.com/504661/why-etsy-engineers-send-company-wide-emails-confessing-mistakes-they-made/. Emphasis added.

8. Amy C. Edmondson, "Building a Psychologically Safe Workplace," TEDx Talks, accessed April 5, 2022, https://www.youtube.com/watch?v=LhoLuui9gX8.

9. William Kahn, "Psychological Conditions of Personal Engagement and Disengagement at Work," *Academy of Management Journal* 33, no. 4 (1990): 692–724.

10. Edgar H. Schein and Warren Bennis, *Personal and Organizational Change via Group Methods* (New York: Wiley, 1965).

11. Amy C. Edmondson, *The Fearless Organization: Creating Psychological Safety in the Workplace for Learning, Innovation, and Growth* (Hoboken, NJ: Wiley, 2018). Also see Laura Delizonna, "High-Performing Teams Need Psychological Safety. Here's How to Create It," *Harvard Business Review*, August 24, 2017, https://hbr.org/2017/08/high-performing-teams-need-psychological-safety-heres-how-to-create-it.

12. "The 4 Stages of Psychological Safety," LeaderFactor, accessed March 8, 2022, https://www.leaderfactor.com/4-stages-of-psychological-safety. Also see Schein and Bennis, *Personal and Organizational Change via Group Methods*.

13. James Shore and Diana Larsen, "The Agile Fluency® Model: A Brief Guide to Success with Agile," 2018, https://www.martinfowler.com/articles/agileFluency.html.

Chapter 3

1. Peter F. Drucker, *Management: Tasks, Responsibilities, Practices* (New York: Harper and Row, 1974), p. 57.

2. Arie de Gues, *The Living Company: Habits for Survival in a Turbulent Business Environment* (Boston: Harvard Business Review Press, 2002), p. 157.

3. Gallup, *State of the Global Workplace: 2021*, https://www.gallup.com/workplace/349484/state-of-the-global-workplace.aspx, p. 7.

4. Ibid.

5. John R. Katzenbach and Douglas K. Smith, *The Wisdom of Teams: Creating the High-Performance Organization* (Boston: Harvard Business Review Press, 2015).

Chapter 4

1. "Continuous Improvement," American Society for Quality, accessed March 8, 2022, https://asq.org/quality-resources/continuous -improvement.

2. Melissa Daimler, "Why Leadership Development Has to Happen on the Job," *Harvard Business Review*, March 16, 2016, https://hbr.org/2016 /03/why-leadership-development-has-to-happen-on-the-job.

3. Carol S. Dweck, *Mindset: The New Psychology of Success* (New York: Ballantine Books, 2007).

4. Adam Grant, *Think Again: The Power of Knowing What You Don't Know* (New York: Viking, 2021), p. 47.

5. Chip R. Bell, "Great Leaders Learn Out Loud," American Management Association, January 24, 2019, https://www.amanet.org/articles /great-leaders-learn-out-loud/.

6. Rosamund Stone Zander and Benjamin Zander, *The Art of Possibility: Transforming Professional and Personal Life* (New York: Penguin Books, 2002).

7. Alistair Cockburn, personal communication with authors.

8. Willem Larsen and Diana Larsen, *The Five Rules of Accelerated Learning* (Leanpub, 2014), https://leanpub.com/fiverules.

9. Drew Bryan, personal communication with authors.

Chapter 5

1. Norman L. Kerth, *Project Retrospectives: A Handbook for Team Review* (New York: Dorset House, 2001), p. 7.

2. "Hindsight Bias," Wikipedia, last edited April 2, 2022, https://en .wikipedia.org/wiki/Hindsight_bias.

3. Esther Derby and Diana Larsen, *Agile Retrospectives: Making Good Teams Great* (Dallas: Pragmatic Bookshelf, 2006).

4. Dale Hunter, *The Art of Facilitation: The Essentials for Leading Great Meetings and Creating Group Synergy* (New York: Random House, 2012), p. 19.

5. Ingrid Bens, *Advanced Facilitation Strategies: Tools and Techniques to Master Difficult Situations* (San Francisco: Jossey-Bass, 2005), p. 16.

6. "Facilitator," Wikipedia, last edited August 26, 2021, https://en .wikipedia.org/wiki/Facilitator.

7. Roger M. Schwarz, *The Skilled Facilitator: A Comprehensive Resource for Consultants, Facilitators, Coaches, and Trainers* (San Francisco: Jossey-Bass, 2016), p. 5.

8. Sam Kaner, *Facilitator's Guide to Participatory Decision-Making* (San Francisco: Jossey-Bass, 2014), p. 32.

9. Schwarz, *The Skilled Facilitator*, p. 40.

10. Edward De Bono, *Six Thinking Hats* (Boston: Back Bay Books, 1999).

11. Ibid.

Part Two

1. Tony Lambert, personal communication with authors.

Chapter 6

1. "Motivation, trust, and safety activity," from Diana Larsen's collection, created by a workshop group in 2004.

2. Private conversation with George Dinwiddie at Retrospective Facilitators Gathering, 2013, Kill Devil Hills, NC.

3. Emily Anhalt (@dremilyanhalt), Twitter, February 24, 2021, https://twitter.com/dremilyanhalt/status/1364613710086479878.

4. Diana Larsen and Ainsley Nies, *Liftoff: Start and Sustain Successful Agile Teams* (Raleigh, NC: Pragmatic Bookshelf, 2012), pp. 41–51.

5. Laura Whitworth, Henry Kimsey-House, Karen Kimsey-House, and Phillip Sandahl, *Co-Active Coaching: New Skills for Coaching People toward Success in Work and Life,* 2nd ed. (Mountain View, CA: Davies-Black, 2007), pp. 31–40.

6. Larsen and Nies, *Liftoff*; Jean Tabaka, *Collaboration Explained: Facilitation Skills for Software Project Leaders* (Upper Saddle River, NJ: Addison-Wesley Professional, 2006); Marsha Acker, *The Art and Science of Facilitation: How to Lead Effective Collaboration with Agile Teams* (Team-Catapult, 2021); Paul Goddard, *Improv-ing Agile Teams: Using Constraints to Unlock Creativity* (Bradford-on-Avon, UK: Agilify, 2019); Keith Sawyer, *Group Genius: The Creative Power of Collaboration* (New York: Basic Books, 2008).

7. Kari Rusnak, "The Magic Ratio: The Key to Relationship Satisfaction," Gottman Institute, accessed March 8, 2022, https://www.gottman.com/blog/the-magic-ratio-the-key-to-relationship-satisfaction/.

8. In 1999 the term *Big Visible Chart* was coined by Kent Beck in *Extreme Programming Explained: Embracing Change* (Boston: Addison-Wesley, 1999) though it was later attributed by Beck to Martin Fowler. In 2001 the term *information radiator* was coined by Alistair Cockburn in his book, *Agile Software Development* (Boston: Addison-Wesley, 2001).

9. Data Therapy, "Activity: Pass-Around Collaborative Drawing," blog post, accessed April 15, 2022, https://datatherapy.org/activities/activity -pass-around-collaborative-drawing/.

10. Sharon L. Bowman, "60-Second Shout-Outs: A 'Got a Minute' Activity from *The Ten-Minute Trainer*," accessed April 15, 2022, https:// bowperson.com/wp-content/uploads/2014/11/60SecondShoutOuts.pdf.

11. Liz Williams, "The 'Yes, and' Icebreaker," Collaboration Zone, accessed April 15, 2022, https://collaborationzone.com/the-yes-and -icebreaker/; "1-2-4-All," Liberating Structures, accessed March 8, 2022, https://www.liberatingstructures.com/1-1-2-4-all/.

12. "Hypothesis activity," Northern Arizona University, accessed April 15, 2022, https://www2.nau.edu/~gaud/bio301/disc.htm.

13. Elva Redwood, "Hurtful Relationship Patterns and Deep Dreams," Process Works Institute, March 7, 2021, https://www.processwork.edu /tag/processwork/.

14. GeePaw Hill, "Many More Much Smaller Steps," blog, September– December 2021, https://www.geepawhill.org/series/many-much-more -smaller-steps/.

Chapter 7

1. See more on Diana's figure in the book by James Shore, with Diana Larsen, Gitte Klitgaard, and Shane Warden, *The Art of Agile Development*, 2nd ed. (Sebastopol, CA: O'Reilly Media, 2021), pp. 290–291.

2. Adapted from Lyssa Adkins, *Coaching Agile Teams: A Companion for ScrumMasters, Agile Coaches, and Project Managers in Transition* (Boston: Addison-Wesley Professional, 2010) and original source Speed Leas.

3. Kimberly Holland, "10 Defense Mechanisms: What Are They and How They Help Us Cope," Healthline, February 11, 2019, https://www .healthline.com/health/mental-health/defense-mechanisms.

4. Danielle Young, "Trauma and the Brain: Signs You Might be Living in 'Survival Mode,'" Child Guidance, June 12, 2020, https://cgrc.org /blog/trauma-and-the-brain-signs-you-might-be-in-survival-mode/.

5. From Diana Larsen and Esther Derby, "Secrets of Agile Teamwork" workshop materials, copyright 2005, 2022.

6. See Luke Hohmann, *Innovation Games: Creating Breakthrough Products through Collaborative Play* (Addison-Wesley Professional, 2006).

7. See Tony Buzan, *How to Mind Map* (London: HarperCollins, 2002).

8. Esther Derby, "5 Sources of Team Conflict," Ether Derby's professional website, March 30, 2011, https://www.estherderby.com/team-trap-3-failing-to-navigate-conflict/.

Chapter 8

1. Diversity, Equity, Inclusion website, accessed March 8, 2022, https://diversityequityinclusion.com/dei-defnined/.

2. Juliet Bourke et al., "Diversity and Inclusion: The Reality Gap," Deloitte Insights, February 28, 2017, https://www2.deloitte.com/us/en/insights/focus/human-capital-trends/2017/diversity-and-inclusion-at-the-workplace.html.

3. Kimberlé Williams Crenshaw, "Demarginalizing the Intersection of Race and Sex: A Black Feminist Critique of Antidiscrimination Doctrine, Feminist Theory and Antiracist Politics," *University of Chicago Legal Forum* 1989, no. 1 (1989): 139–167.

4. N. N. Johnson and T. L. Johnson, "Microaggressions: An Introduction," in *Navigating Micro-Aggressions Toward Women in Higher Education*, ed. U. Thomas, pp. 1–22 (IGI Global), https://doi:10.4018/978-1-5225-5942-9. See also "The Forgotten Tale of How Black Psychiatrists Helped Make 'Sesame Street,'" *The Daily Beast,* updated May 19, 2019, https://www.thedailybeast.com/chester-pierce-the-forgotten-tale-of-how-a-black-psychiatrist-helped-make-sesame-street.

5. D. W. Sue, C. M Capodilupo, G. C. Torino, J. M. Bucceri, A. M. B. Holder, A. M. B., K. L. Nadal, and M. Esquilin, "Racial Microaggressions in Everyday Life: Implications for Clinical Practice." *American Psychologist* 62, no. 4 (2007): 271.

6. "Implicit Stereotype," Wikipedia, last edited March 15, 2022, https://en.wikipedia.org/wiki/Implicit_stereotype.

7. From Diane J. Goodman, "Responding to Biased or Offensive Comments," 2011, https://dianegoodman.com/wp-content/uploads/2020/05/RespondingToBiasedOrOffensiveCommentsexcerptarticle.pdf.

. Dolly Chugh, *The Person You Mean to Be: How Good People Fight Bias* New York: Harper Business, 2018), pp. 232–233.

9. Adapted from Adam Grant, *Think Again: The Power of Knowing What You Don't Know* (New York: Viking, 2021).

10. "Dunning–Kruger Effect," Wikipedia, last edited March 19, 2022, https://en.wikipedia.org/wiki/Dunning–Kruger_effect.

11. "Imposter Syndrome," Wikipedia, last edited April 4, 2022, https://en.wikipedia.org/wiki/Impostor_syndrome.

12. Derald Wing Sue, *Race Talk and the Conspiracy of Silence: Understanding and Facilitating Difficult Dialogues on Race* (Hoboken, NJ: Wiley, 2016), pp. 186–205.

13. Malik Miah, "John Lewis: 'Never Be Afraid to Get in Good Trouble, Necessary Trouble,'" Greenleft, July 26, 2020, https://www.greenleft.org.au /content/john-lewis-never-be-afraid-get-good-trouble-necessary-trouble. .

14. Chugh, *Person You Mean to Be*, p. 135.

15. "Individual silent writing brainstorming," University of Sheffield, accessed April 22, 2022, https://www.sheffield.ac.uk/polopoly_fs/1 .470010!/file/HowtoReverseBrainstorming.pdf.

16. American Society for Quality, "Force Field Analysis," accessed April 15, 2022, https://asq.org/quality-resources/force-field-analysis.

17. Board of Innovation, "Evaluation Criteria," accessed April 19, 2022, https://www.boardofinnovation.com/tools/evaluation-criteria/.

18. Esther Derby and Diana Larsen, "Activity: Check-in," in *Agile Retrospectives: Making Good Teams Great* (Raleigh, NC: Pragmatic Bookshelf, 2006), pp. 40–41.

Chapter 9

1. Center for Right Relationship (CRR) Global, Fundamentals of ORSC course training materials.

2. "Groupthink," Wikipedia, last edited April 4, 2022, https://en .wikipedia.org/wiki/Groupthink.

3. Ruth Tam, "Leadership at Work Is an Art Form. Here's How to Practice It," *Life Kit*, NPR, July 20, 2021, https://www.npr.org/2021/07/19 /1017946868/leadership-work-manager-career-development.

4. Lyssa Adkins, "Constellations," in *Coaching Agile Teams: A Companion for ScrumMasters, Agile Coaches, and Project Managers in Transition* (Boston: Addison-Wesley Professional, 2010), pp. 155–157.

5. Jean Tabaka, "Consensus Check: The Fist of Five," in *Collaboration Explained : Facilitation Skills for Software Project Leaders* (Indianapolis: Addison-Wesley, 2006), pp. 80–81.

Conclusion

1. Simon Sinek, *The Infinite Game* (New York: Penguin/Portfolio, 2019), p. 129.

2. Brian Stanfield, ed., *The Art of Focused Conversation: 100 Ways to Access Group Wisdom in the Workplace* (Gabriola Island, BC: New Society Publishers, 2000), pp. 22–30.

3. Sherri Mandell, *The Road to Resilience: From Chaos to Celebration* (New Milford, CT: The Toby Press, 2015).

Bibliography

Adkins, Lyssa. *Coaching Agile Teams: A Companion for ScrumMasters, Agile Coaches, and Project Managers in Transition*. Boston: Addison-Wesley Professional, 2010.

Beck, Kent. *Extreme Programming Explained: Embracing Change*. Boston: Addison-Wesley, 1999.

Bell, Chip R. "Great Leaders Learn Out Loud." American Management Association, January 24, 2019. https://www.amanet.org/articles/great -leaders-learn-out-loud/.

Buzan, Tony. *How to Mind Map*. London: HarperCollins, 2002.

Cockburn, Alistair. *Agile Software Development*. Boston: Addison-Wesley, 2001.

De Bono, Edward. *Six Thinking Hats*. Boston: Back Bay Books, 1999.

Delizonna, Laura. "High-Performing Teams Need Psychological Safety. Here's How to Create It." *Harvard Business Review*, August 24, 2017, https://hbr.org/2017/08/high-performing-teams-need-psychological -safety-heres-how-to-create-it.

Denning, Steve. "The Dumbest Idea in the World: Maximizing Shareholder Value." *Forbes*, November 28, 2011. https://www.forbes.com /sites/stevedenning/2011/11/28/maximizing-shareholder-value-the -dumbest-idea-in-the-world/?sh=354420822870.

Drucker, Peter F. "Knowledge-Worker Productivity: The Biggest Challenge." *California Management Review* 41, no. 2 (1999): 79–94. doi:10.2307 /41165987.

Edmondson, Amy C. *The Fearless Organization: Creating Psychological Safety in the Workplace for Learning, Innovation, and Growth*. Hoboken, NJ: Wiley, 2018.

Hohmann, Luke. *Innovation Games: Creating Breakthrough Products through Collaborative Play*. Boston: Addison-Wesley Professional, 2006.

Johnson, N. N., and T. L. Johnson. "Microaggressions: An Introduction," in *Navigating Micro-Aggressions Toward Women in Higher Education*,

ed. U. Thomas, pp. 1–22. IGI Global, https://doi:10.4018/978-1-5225
-5942-9.ch001.

Kahn, William. "Psychological Conditions of Personal Engagement and Disengagement at Work." *Academy of Management Journal* 33, no. 4 (1990): 692–724.

Leybourn, Evan, and Shane Hastie. *#noprojects: A Culture of Continuous Value.* lulu.com, 2019.

Mandell, Sherri. *The Road to Resilience: From Chaos to Celebration.* New Milford, CT: The Toby Press, 2015.

Marquet, L. David. *Turn the Ship Around! A True Story of Turning Followers into Leaders.* New York: Portfolio, 2013.

MIT Sloan Management Review. "Why Our Minds Swap Out Hard Questions for Easy Ones." December 22, 2011. https://sloanreview.mit.edu /article/why-our-minds-swap-out-hard-questions-for-easy-ones/.

Schein, Edgar, and Warren Bennis. *Personal and Organizational Change via Group Methods.* New York: Wiley, 1965.

Schein, Edgar, and Peter Schein. *Humble Leadership.* Oakland, CA: Berrett-Koehler, 2018.

———. *Humble Inquiry.* 2nd ed. Oakland, CA: Berrett-Koehler, 2021.

Senge, Peter M. *The Fifth Discipline: The Art & Practice of The Learning Organization.* New York: Currency, 2006.

Shore, James. *The Art of Agile Development,* 2nd ed. Sebastopol, CA: O'Reilly Media, 2021.

Sinek, Simon. *The Infinite Game.* New York: Penguin/Portfolio, 2019.

Snowden, Dave, and Riva Greenberg, *Cynefin—Weaving Sense-Making into the Fabric of Our World.* Singapore: Cognitive Edge—The Cynefin Co., 2020.

Stanfield, Brian, ed. *The Art of Focused Conversation : 100 Ways to Access Group Wisdom in the Workplace.* Gabriola Island, BC: New Society Publishers, 2000.

Sue, Derald Wing. *Race Talk and the Conspiracy of Silence: Understanding and Facilitating Difficult Dialogues on Race.* Hoboken, NJ: Wiley, 2016.

Sue, D. W., C. M Capodilupo, G. C. Torino, J. M. Bucceri, A. M. B. Holder, A. M. B., K. L. Nadal, and M. Esquilin, "Racial Microaggressions in Everyday Life: Implications for Clinical Practice." *American Psychologist* 62, no. 4 (2007): 271.

Whitworth, Laura, Henry Kimsey-House, Karen Kimsey-House, and Phillip Sandahl. *Co-Active Coaching: New Skills for Coaching People toward Success in Work and Life,* 2nd ed. Mountain View, CA: Davies-Black, 2007.

Appreciations

Writing this book challenged our collaboration and our thinking. We want to honor the industry experts and authors who influenced our thinking, our abilities, and our own leadership experiences. Much of the work that we do has been collaborative over the years. We've worked with many partners, and we've both drawn on many sources of knowledge. We appreciate the contributions from the numerous references we've included in this book. Wherever possible, we cite our sources. We've done our best to ensure that no sources are accidently misattributed or missed. However, it's inevitable that we have overlooked someone or some source. We apologize up front for any acknowledgment that fails to meet the high standard we attempted.

We worked with a terrific team at Berrett-Koehler, especially our editor Charlotte Ashlock. Charlotte's insistence and vision helped motivate us to create and deliver what we didn't even know needed to be said. During a time of chaos, this team was resilient in helping us get this message out.

We are incredibly lucky to have the support of several colleagues and friends who contributed to this book through valuable conversations and insightful review feedback: Drew Bryan, Jake Calabrese, Todd Christian, Anthony Coppedge, Angie Drumm, Jim Dusseau, Tamani George, Peter Green, Kellie Kennedy, Tony Lambert, Willem Larsen, Lissa Millspaugh, Heidi Muesser, Stephanie Norton, Allison Pollard, Christopher Richardson, and David Slick.

As neither of us is graphically inclined, we are grateful for talented families. Thank you to Abby Larsen and Peter Broderick, wonderful designers who were willing to help us with key illustrations.

We are grateful to Esther Derby and Van Williams for contributing forewords to this book. You both are wonderful examples of learning leaders who make a difference.

Diana Larsen's Acknowledgments

Foremost, I acknowledge my writing partner and colleague, Tricia Broderick. I intended to write another book. I'd been asked. I even wanted to write another book (or a few). Yet I stalled. I knew that I get the most enjoyment and learning from writing when I have a good collaborator. In Tricia, I found another great match as a coauthor. As we uncovered what we wanted and needed to say together, we shifted our relationship. We grew from colleagues in the agile community to dear and valued friends. We have produced something publishable from our effort. Even so, our relationship alone would have been a most satisfying recompense.

Writing a book takes time and energy. As I entered 2021, I found myself with an overabundance of writing projects. More projects than any sane person would take on at once. Somehow it worked out. I appreciate all the colleagues who gave me forbearance and grace. That allowed me to persevere through the year with relationships and responsibilities intact. They all kept me moving forward. Those colleagues include Wolf-Gideon Bleek, Esther Derby, David Horowitz, Tommi Johnstone, James Shore, Michael Tardiff, and the AgilePDX Agile Coaching Qualities team—Nora Sunhilt Beyerle, Diane Brady, Craig Carrington, Lori Gordon, Michaela Hutfles, Sean Lemson, and Neal Petersen—as well as all those others who have offered feedback along the way. Onward!

To all the giants with sturdy, insightful, and generous shoulders, I send out my gratitude. I have benefited from the acumen of other writers, speakers, and discussion partners in many fields. The practices of organization development, organization design, and change management; leadership/management and team development; complexity, chaos, and systems theory; Lean, Flow, Business Agility, and agile; and many more. We've called out many individuals in the pages of this book and the references. I have particular appreciation for the work of Edgar Schein, who continues to contribute valuable new leadership ideas building on his vast experience. There are many more. Without a community of researchers and thinkers, coaches, consultants, and mentors, both side by side and at distance, this work could not go forward.

To family and friends who have supported, encouraged, flattered, loved, shaken, and challenged me, you have my greatest thanks.

Tricia Broderick's Acknowledgments

As someone who speaks about challenging yourself to come out of your comfort zone, cowriting a book checked all the boxes for triggering my insecurities. Every time I thought, "This is crazy," I leaned on an amazing community that lifted me back up. I'll never be able to thank everyone enough for helping me along this journey.

For many years, I had known and respected Diana Larsen. Throughout this entire process, I could have easily put myself in a supporting role to Diana. I mean, she's Diana Larsen! But she always engaged with me as a partner. Even when I tried to let informal power come into play, she demonstrated every bit of the learning leader she is. I'm proud of what we created. But the absolute best part was deepening our conversations, care, and relationship. Thank you, Diana, for choosing to do this with me.

To Esther Derby and Mike Cohn: Years ago, when I was slowly considering writing a book, you both gave wonderful advice. It may have taken me a while, but I did listen. In fact, there were times that I had to replay your words to get past my fears. Thank you.

There are two professional parts of my life that have greatly influenced my leadership: all the colleagues whom I've had the honor of working with, and the agile community that believes in people first. I thrive on connections. They help me learn. They help me be inspired. They help me rebuild energy. Whether the experience was intense collaboration, a deep exploration of a challenging issue, or dancing our hearts out, I carry these moments with me. To list every single person for whom I'm grateful, well, that is an entire book in itself. So instead, to each one of you, thank you for helping me become a leader.

To my family and friends, I am here today because of your love and support. In 2005 I thought my passion for being a leader was gone. My family and friends helped me realize that I really needed to evolve my career purpose. That who I was personally wasn't who was showing up in the workplace. My family and friends helped me find the courage to be truly authentic. To focus on making a difference for people through leadership. Again, this list is too long to highlight each name, and I selfishly don't want to risk missing anyone. But you know who you are—you have to deal with me constantly! I truly have amazing people in my corner, and you have my utmost appreciation. Always.

Index

Note: Page numbers followed by *t* or *f* indicate a table or figure on the designated page.

About the Authors

Visionary pragmatist **Diana Larsen** is a cofounder, chief connector, learning leader, and principal coach, consultant, and mentor at the Agile Fluency Project. Diana coauthored the books *Agile Retrospectives: Making Good Teams Great*; *Liftoff: Start and Sustain Successful Agile Teams*; and *Five Rules of Accelerated Learning*. She co-originated the Agile Fluency model and coauthored the book *The Agile Fluency Model: A Brief Guide to Success with Agile*. For more than 20 years, she led the practice area for agile software development, leading and managing teams, and guiding agile transitions at FutureWorks Consulting. The continuing thread in her career has been a focus on group learning and leaders who "learn out loud" to support their teams and organizations.

Since 2015 she has devoted her energy to a new endeavor. Through the Agile Fluency Project's programs for training, mentoring, and supporting agile coaches and consultants, Diana shares the wisdom she's gained in over 35 years of working with leaders, teams, and organizations. To serve her communities, she delivers inspiring conference keynotes, talks, and workshops around the world.

Tricia Broderick is a leadership adviser and motivational speaker. With more than 25 years of experience, Tricia embraces vulnerability to share her learnings from a wide range of industries, including independent software vendors, financial services, government, energy, education, and gaming. Tricia holds a bachelor of computer science and engineering from Michigan State University. She began this journey as a software engineer. Later, she evolved into roles such as project manager, functional manager, team lead, director of development, executive, trainer, and coach.

As a learning leader, Tricia boldly prioritizes people and connections. Her aim is to amplify inclusive collaborations that challenge and support people's learning in an authentic and engaging way. She founded Ignite Insight + Innovation to help ignite leaders and teams toward truly achieving resiliency. As an influential leader in the agile community, industry experts recognize Tricia's contributions. Linda Rising, coauthor of *Fearless Change* and *More Fearless Change*, says, "Tricia opened my eyes to a lot of nuance about people, about leadership, about training, about listening, about learning, that I can honestly say have stayed with me as helpful maxims ever since. I never miss a chance to learn from Tricia!" Mike Cohn, author of *Succeeding with Agile*, says, "Tricia is a wealth of ideas in getting people to fully understand being agile and its many subtleties. When I wanted to improve my own courses, I thought first and only of Tricia and her suggestions improved my training courses."

When not traveling to speak at events and experience the world, Tricia lives in the Denver, Colorado, area with her family.

G ilmara Vila Nova-Mitchell is a diversity, equity, and inclusion consultant and the IMT Insurance DEI director. She is on a mission to put people first in the workplace and help others do the same. Born in Brazil, Gilmara began to develop an interest in DEI when she immigrated to the United States. Her personal experiences as an immigrant and a woman of color greatly affected her perspective on inclusion. As she designed organizational systems that attended to all people, Gilmara learned firsthand that inclusive leadership was an essential component of any organization's success.

Gilmara holds a bachelor of multicultural education from FUMEC University (Brazil) and a master in education in school counseling from Drake University. She has completed doctoral studies in organizational development with a focus on trust in the workplace. For almost two decades, Gilmara has helped organizations become more inclusive through her engaging DEI sessions, transformative executive coaching, and innovative systems redesign. She is also a proud mama to two incredible, strong, and fierce daughters.